Panorama of the New Testament

Stephen J. Binz

with Little Rock Scripture Study staff

Little Rock
Scripture Study

A ministry of the Diocese of Little Rock
in partnership with Liturgical Press

Nihil Obstat for the commentary text by Stephen J. Binz: Reverend Robert C. Harren, J.C.L., *Censor deputatus.*
Imprimatur for the commentary text by Stephen J. Binz: ✛ Most Reverend Donald J. Kettler, J.C.L., Bishop of
St. Cloud, Minnesota. June 7, 2016.

Cover design by Ann Blattner. Interior art by Ned Bustard.

This symbol indicates material that was created by Little Rock Scripture Study to supplement the
biblical text and commentary. Some of these inserts first appeared in the *Little Rock Catholic Study
Bible*; others were created specifically for this book by Amy Ekeh.

1   2   3   4   5   6   7   8   9

Library of Congress Cataloging-in-Publication Data

Library of Congress Control number: 2018956719

ISBN 978-0-8146-6374-5   ISBN 978-0-8146-6398-1 (e-book)

Office of the Bishop

DIOCESE OF LITTLE ROCK

2500 North Tyler Street • P.O. Box 7565 • Little Rock, Arkansas 72217 • (501) 664-0340 Fax (501) 664-6304

Dear Friends,

The Bible is a gift of God to the church, the people gathered around the world throughout the ages in the name of Christ. God uses this sacred writing to continue to speak to us in all times and places.

I encourage you to make it your own by dedicated prayer and study with others and on your own. Little Rock Scripture Study is a ministry of the Catholic Diocese of Little Rock. It provides the tools you need to faithfully understand what you are reading, to appreciate its meaning for you and for our world, and to guide you in a way that will deepen your own ability to respond to God's call.

It is my hope that the Word of God will empower you as Christians to live a life worthy of your call as a child of God.

Sincerely in Christ,

✠ Anthony B. Taylor
Bishop of Little Rock

TABLE OF CONTENTS

Wrap-up lectures are available for each lesson at no charge. The link to these free lectures is LittleRockScripture.org/Lectures/PanoramaNewTestament.

Welcome

The Bible is at the heart of what it means to be a Christian. It is the Spirit-inspired word of God for us. It reveals to us the God who created, redeemed, and guides us still. It speaks to us personally and as a church. It forms the basis of our public liturgical life and our private prayer lives. It urges us to live worthily and justly, to love tenderly and wholeheartedly, and to be a part of building God's kingdom here on earth.

Though it was written a long time ago, in the context of a very different culture, the Bible is no relic of the past. Catholic biblical scholarship is among the best in the world, and in our time and place, we have unprecedented access to it. By making use of solid scholarship, we can discover much about the ancient culture and religious practices that shaped those who wrote the various books of the Bible. With these insights, and by praying with the words of Scripture, we allow the words and images to shape us as disciples. By sharing our journey of faithful listening to God's word with others, we have the opportunity to be stretched in our understanding and to form communities of love and learning. Ultimately, studying and praying with God's word deepens our relationship with Christ.

Panorama of the New Testament

The resource you hold in your hands is divided into four lessons. Each lesson involves personal prayer and study using this book *and* the experience of group prayer, discussion, and wrap-up lecture.

If you are using this resource in the context of a small group, we suggest that you meet four times, discussing one lesson per meeting. Allow about 90 minutes for the small group gathering. Small groups function best with eight to twelve people to ensure good group dynamics and to allow all to participate as they wish.

WHAT MATERIALS WILL YOU USE?

The materials in this book include:

- Commentary by Stephen J. Binz, which has also been published separately as *Panorama of the Bible: New Testament* (Liturgical Press).

- Occasional inserts  highlighting elements of the New Testament. Some of these appear also in the *Little Rock*

Catholic Study Bible while others are supplied by staff writers.

- Questions for study, reflection, and discussion at the end of each lesson.

- Opening and closing prayers for each lesson, as well as other prayer forms available in the closing pages of the book.

In addition, there are wrap-up lectures available for each lesson. Your group may choose to purchase a DVD containing these lectures or make use of the audio or video lectures online at no charge. The link to these free lectures is: LittleRockScripture.org/Lectures/PanoramaNewTestament. Of course, if your group has access to qualified speakers, you may choose to have live presentations.

Each person will need a current translation of the Bible. We recommend the *Little Rock Catholic Study Bible*, which makes use of the New American Bible, Revised Edition. Other translations, such as the New Jerusalem Bible or the New Revised Standard Version: Catholic Edition, would also work well.

HOW WILL YOU USE THESE MATERIALS?

Prepare in advance

Using Lesson One as an example:

- Begin with a simple prayer like the one found on page 11.

- Read the assigned material in the printed book for Lesson One (pages 12–31) so that you are prepared for the weekly small group session. You may do this assignment by reading a portion over a period of several days (effective and manageable) or by preparing all at once (more challenging).

- Answer the questions, Exploring Lesson One, found at the end of the assigned reading, pages 32–34.

- Use the Closing Prayer on page 34 when you complete your study. This prayer may be used again when you meet with the group.

Meet with your small group

- After introductions and greetings, allow time for prayer (about 5 minutes) as you begin the group session. You may use the prayer found on page 11 (also used by individuals in their preparation) or use a prayer of your choosing.

- Spend about 45–50 minutes discussing the responses to the questions that were prepared in advance. You may also develop your discussion further by responding to questions and interests that arise during the discussion and faith-sharing itself.

- Close the discussion and faith-sharing with prayer, about 5–10 minutes. You may use the Closing Prayer at the end of each lesson or one of your choosing at the end of the book. It is important to allow people to pray for personal and community needs and to give thanks for how God is moving in your lives.

- Listen to or view the wrap-up lecture associated with each lesson (15–20 minutes). You may watch the lecture online, use a DVD, or provide a live lecture by a qualified local speaker. This lecture provides a common focus for the group and reinforces insights from each lesson. You may view the lecture together at the end of the session or, if your group runs out of time, you may invite group members to watch the lecture on their own time after the discussion.

Above all, be aware that the Holy Spirit is moving within and among you.

Panorama of the New Testament

LESSON ONE

The Gospels of Matthew and Mark

Begin your personal study and group discussion with a simple and sincere prayer such as:

Prayer

Jesus Christ, you are the Word that reveals the Father. As we study the good news of your life, death, and resurrection, may what you reveal to us take root in our hearts and give life to our church and to our world.

Read the Preface and pages 12–31, Lesson One.

Respond to the questions on pages 32–34, Exploring Lesson One.

The Closing Prayer on page 34 is for your personal use and may be used at the end of group discussion.

PREFACE

As we continue this panorama of the Bible, moving into the New Testament, we continue to survey the narrative of God's people from Genesis to Revelation, from creation to the renewal of all things in the new creation for which we are destined. This story of God's family told around the table is essentially one unfolding drama. Although we are tempted to think that the New Testament moves us to an altogether new story with new themes and a new plot, we will see that the same themes are interwoven through both testaments and that the same plot that began to develop in Genesis carries on through the life of Jesus and his church.

We will continue to view the big picture so as to understand how the whole Bible fits together. Set against the backdrop of God's design for creation and of human rebellion against that design, the New Testament continues and completes the narrative of God's redemption of the world. The wide variety of books and types of literature in the New Testament continue to tell the one story of salvation.

Learning to take this panoramic view of the Bible, we are better able to understand that this is our story. We can enter into the narrative more personally and view our lives as participants in this great drama of salvation. The better we grasp the big picture and the whole narrative, the better we will embody Scripture, find our own place in the story, and become participants in the mission of God.

The biblical scholar N. T. Wright describes the Bible and our role within it with an analogy. He imagines that the script of a lost Shakespearean play is somehow discovered. Although the play originally had five acts, only a little more than four have been found—the first four acts and the first scene of act five. The rest is missing. The play is given to Shakespear-

ean actors who are asked to work out the rest of act five for themselves. Immersing themselves in Shakespearean language and in the narrative of the partial script that has been recovered, they improvise the missing parts of the fifth act, allowing their performance to be shaped by the trajectory of the story as they have come to understand it. In this way they bring the work toward the conclusion that its author had indicated previously in the play.[†]

Wright says that this analogy may help us understand how the Bible can shape our own lives now. The biblical drama of redemption unfolds in five acts: (1) creation, (2) the fall into sin, (3) Israel's story, (4) the story of Jesus, and (5) the story of the church, leading to the consummation of God's plan of redemption. We know that the Author of the drama, the Divine "Playwright," has given the gift of his own Spirit to the "actors." So we must live our lives within the trajectory of the story as it has been told up to the first part of the final act. We have been entrusted to perform the continuation of the biblical drama within the mission of Jesus and his church, moving the story forward to the conclusion that God has already imagined.

We are each invited to enter into the plot as it stands, continually poring over and immersing ourselves in the earlier acts, and learning to understand how the threads can be drawn together. We then improvise, speaking and acting creatively, yet in a way consistent with the story of Israel, Jesus, and the early church. We each imaginatively yet faithfully live out the narrative impetus given in Scripture in the new historical and cultural situations in which our lives are placed by God.

Standing as we do between Pentecost and the completion of God's plan for creation, our mission is to witness to the reign of God over the whole world. When we understand that the Bible is our literature, we can better recognize how we fit into this great story of God and humanity. As we survey in this volume the

[†] N. T. Wright, *The New Testament and the People of God*, Christian Origins and the Question of God 1 (Minneapolis: Fortress, 1992), 143.

story of Jesus and the story of his early church, we will comprehend ever more clearly how our individual lives are being shaped by this inspired literature and how we are each being molded into the persons we are created to be.

As we grasp how the world's redemption has been accomplished in Jesus, we will understand the mission of the church and our own mission within it to participate in God's bringing redemption to its completion.

THE GOOD NEWS OF JESUS CHRIST

On the third day following the crucifixion of Jesus in Jerusalem, two disciples are traveling on the road to Emmaus, talking to each other about his life and death. Despite the teachings of Jesus, they have failed to comprehend how the narrative of his life continues the narrative of Israel from the Scriptures. They are "slow of heart" to believe what the prophets spoke, failing to understand the drama of redemption, so they are filled with gloom and despair.

Then the risen Jesus joins the two disciples on the road and responds to their hopeless state. He takes the disciples back through the Scriptures of Israel, showing them God's purpose and plan: "Then beginning with Moses and all the prophets, he interpreted to them what referred to him in all the scriptures" (Luke 24:27). Jesus provides the interpretation of Scripture that relates the ancient texts to himself. He offers them the panoramic view, opening up the plot and showing them how God's saving plan is accomplished in himself.

Jesus' opening the Scriptures to these disciples leads them to the table for Sunday dinner. In the eucharistic meal, their eyes are opened and they recognize their risen Lord. As he vanishes from their sight, they say to each other, "Were not our hearts burning [within us] while he spoke to us on the way and opened the scriptures to us?" (Luke 24:32). In word and sacrament, Jesus has given them an experience of God's saving design for their own lives and for the world.

When these disciples run back to Jerusalem to join the others, Jesus appears to the whole group. Again, in the context of a meal, Jesus says to them, "These are my words that I spoke to you while I was still with you, that everything written about me in the law of Moses and in the prophets and psalms must be fulfilled" (Luke 24:44). Then, the gospel writer says, "He opened their minds to understand the scriptures." The risen Lord, gathered with his disciples, shows them how he is the heart and center of the great narrative of Scripture.

The Torah, the prophets, and the psalms are all filled with anticipation of the Messiah. The Old Testament is most fully understood in the light of Christ; and the significance of Jesus and the meaning of his life can be seen only through these ancient texts. With their minds open to understanding and their hearts on fire, the disciples are now able to see the big picture—the panorama of Scripture.

The Good News of God's Redemption

Although God is the source and cause of all things, the Creator of the world, God's creation is defiled by rebellion and contaminated by sin. But God has shown a relentless determination to redeem the world, to restore it to what God always intended it to be. The history of ancient Israel tells of God's plan to save all people by choosing one nation as a demonstration of what it means to be in covenant with God. God would free them from bondage, dwell in their midst, reign as their king, and give them a future full of hope. Through this chosen people, God would bring a new creation and the blessings of salvation to all the nations of the world.

Yet, the accomplishment of God's plan continues to be disfigured by the rebellion and sin of his people, and the fulfillment of God's saving will is continually delayed into the future. Israel is taken into exile in Babylon and scattered throughout the earth so that restoration of God's plan seems impossible without a new intervention of God to fulfill the divine promises to Israel and to the world. Beginning with Babylon, as Daniel the prophet has announced, four different kingdoms will rule over God's people until God brings about the coming of his own kingdom. Then the time of the Messiah will put an end to the captivity of God's people and usher in the reign of God.

The prophet Isaiah has kept alive the hope of the exile's end and the new creation that God will accomplish. The beleaguered Jews of first-century Palestine hold these prophecies closely and they recognize when they are being fulfilled. Isaiah evokes the hope of his listeners with the image of a messenger, an evangelizer bringing "good news." Speeding across the mountains, he carries and announces the good news, proclaiming that God's promises are being fulfilled.

> How beautiful upon the mountains
>   are the feet of the one bringing good news,
> Announcing peace, bearing good news,
>   announcing salvation, saying to Zion,
>   "Your God is King!"
> Listen! Your sentinels raise a cry,
>   together they shout for joy,
> For they see directly, before their eyes,
>   the Lord's return to Zion.
> Break out together in song,
>   O ruins of Jerusalem!
> For the Lord has comforted his people,
>   has redeemed Jerusalem.
> The Lord has bared his holy arm
>   in the sight of all the nations;
> All the ends of the earth can see
>   the salvation of our God. (Isa 52:7-10)

The bearer of good news announces the heart of his message, "Your God is King!" And this reign of God brings about "salvation." The scene is one of great joy in which the sentinels on the crumbled walls of Jerusalem and even the ruins themselves form a jubilant chorus.

They see beyond the messenger and realize that the Lord himself is returning to the city to live with his people. God has "comforted" his people, ending their sorrow and bringing relief from their pain and grief. God also has "redeemed" his people, accomplishing their release and restoration.

The good news that God returns, reigns, and redeems will ultimately benefit "all the nations." The good news spreads from the messenger to "all the ends of the earth." The word of God opens outwardly from a word directed to Israel to a word with universal scope. God's word becomes good news for all people, a promise of salvation to the world.

The good news of Isaiah's prophecy is ultimately the good news of Jesus the Messiah. Centuries after Isaiah's prophecy during the exile in Babylon, the words on the ancient scroll of the prophet are now ringing in the ears of the Jewish people. God is returning to rule! Redemption is at hand! The time of salvation has come!

The Kingdom of God Has Come

In the first century, there is a widespread expectation among the Jewish people that God is about to act in order to free his people, renew creation, and bring his reign over the earth. But how are they to live in anticipation of that time? How can they rid themselves of the hated Roman oppressors and hasten the messianic age? What is God asking of them?

Four different answers to these questions take the form of four movements among the Jewish people: the Zealots advocate revolution and overthrow of the Romans; the Sadducees espouse compromise with the Roman authorities; the Pharisees promote cultural and religious separation from the Romans; and the Essenes practice complete withdrawal. But each of these has in common an abhorrence for the Gentiles, an entrenched suspicion of peoples outside of God's covenant with Israel.

The Jews of the first century describe the kingdom of God as a life without subjugation and oppression in which God's peace will reign. In this fullness of time, the forces of evil will be conquered, God's people will be reunited, their sins will be purged and their sickness healed, and a restored and glorified Jerusalem will stand at the heart of the kingdom. The kingdom of God is the time of God's salvation.

Jesus announces that the long wait is over. At the beginning of his public ministry he proclaims: "This is the time of fulfillment. The kingdom of God is at hand. Repent, and believe in the gospel" (Mark 1:15). The kingdom of God is at the heart of Jesus' ministry. It is the time of God's decisive intervention into human history. What the prophets had preached and the people had longed for is now a reality. Jesus casts out demons, works miracles of healing, and calls to himself the outcasts and sinners—all signs that the kingdom of God is at hand, that the final age of God's plan is dawning.

Jesus comes with a marvelously different way from that of the Zealots, Sadducees, Pharisees, and Essenes. His is the way of love of enemies instead of vengeance, readiness to suffer rather than retaliation, unity instead of separation, and engagement rather than withdrawal. It is the path of love, suffering, and peacemaking. His disciples come to recognize that Jesus himself both proclaims and embodies the kingdom of God on earth.

The early church realizes that the kingdom of God is both a present and a future reality. In the life, death, and resurrection of Jesus and in the coming of the Holy Spirit, believers know that God's reign has come. But they also recognize that they still await the full expression of God's kingdom. They already live in the Spirit, but they know that the forces of evil in the world are still alive. They realize that God has been finally and fully manifested in Jesus Christ, yet they are oriented toward the future, when God's promises for all people will be complete.

Despite this future dimension of God's kingdom, its New Testament proclamation is no longer about waiting for the future but about recognizing its presence among us. It focuses on the arrival of the kingdom in Jesus. The distance between God and his people caused by sin and experienced as exile has been eliminated. God is now actively involved in the world and dynamically in relationship with people. The prophets of old, filled with God's spirit, saw it dimly; disciples of Jesus, living in God's kingdom, now see it clearly. What Israel's history had pointed toward has now broken into human history and is made evident in the story of Jesus told by the gospels.

Jesus Gathers a Community

As Jesus announces that the kingdom of God is at hand, he calls individuals to respond with repentance and faith: "Repent, and believe in the gospel." The gospel is the "good news," the joyful announcement, proclaimed by Isaiah's message, that God reigns and has come to bring salvation to the ends of the earth. Repentance means turning from false views of the world and embracing the presence of God's kingdom in Jesus. Believing means trusting that God's liberating and healing power is present in Jesus.

After Jesus' appeal to repent and believe, he issues the invitation to "follow" him. Jesus wants disciples to come and be with him, to learn from him, to become participants in his divine mission in the world. Disciples must center their lives on him with full commitment and total loyalty to God's kingdom.

The people of Israel were called to exist as a nation in covenant with God, but they failed to live this calling and were scattered to the other nations. But through the prophets God promised that Israel would one day be restored and brought together again under God's reign. The growing community of Jesus' disciples is the beginning of restored Israel, the renewal of God's people.

From among his disciples, Jesus deliberately appoints twelve who spend their lives with him. These Twelve, who represent the twelve tribes of Israel, are the nucleus of God's restored people. His choosing them proclaims that God is calling Israel back to the original purpose of God's people. It is a prophetic action that portrays his gathering of the nation. And his later sending out the Twelve to share in his mission expresses the renewal of Israel in the age of God's kingdom.

But the redemption that God brings to his people will not be limited to Israel. Although Israel is the first to be gathered and renewed, all the nations will be gathered to Israel to share in its deliverance. Isaiah develops two prophetic images to describe this universal salvation. First, Israel becomes a great light to which all the people of the world are drawn. God's chosen ones must be this light to the nations, so that God's salvation may reach to the ends of the earth. Second, Israel hosts a great banquet that God provides. This feast of rich food and choice wines is offered for all nations, removing the tears of sorrow and the veil of death from all people.

Jesus will develop these prophetic images of light and feasting as he teaches his disciples. As he opens the kingdom of God to increasingly wider groups of people, he teaches his followers to be witnesses to others, letting their light shine before all people so that all may give praise to God. And as Jesus demonstrates his way of life to his followers, he does so in table fellowship with increasingly more diverse groups. The banquet becomes an image of God's kingdom realized in the eucharistic communion of his church.

Within Jesus' community, he includes a diverse multitude. Among his closest collaborators, Jesus includes a tax collector, who worked for the Roman oppressors, and a zealot, who actively sought to overthrow them. He draws to himself the poor, the sick, and the lost. Sinners and prostitutes are welcome among his company. In his parable of the Great Banquet, the master directs his servants to bring in the poor and the crippled, the blind and the lame. All of the outcasts who are shunned by much of Jewish society are warmly welcomed by Jesus into the kingdom of God.

Jesus Teaches about the Kingdom of God

The kingdom of God that comes into the world with Jesus does not look anything like the kind of military and triumphal monarchy that many expect. When Jesus announces that the kingdom is at hand, nothing major seems to happen. Their world doesn't seem changed much at all by the things that Jesus is saying and doing. The Romans still patrol the streets, the Jews are still oppressed, and no one appears liberated. So the teachings of Jesus, especially his parables, are designed to help his disciples understand the nature of God's kingdom. Jesus tells these parables so that those who repent and believe will learn to comprehend the mystery of the kingdom of God.

First, Jesus says that the kingdom is like the seeding of a field by a farmer (Mark 4:1-12; Luke 8:4-10). Only that seed that lands on fertile soil will grow and produce a harvest. The word of God, like the seed, must be patiently planted in the lives of those who are willing to take away the obstacles to its growth. Although many believed that the Messiah would come with conquering power that no enemy could resist, he comes with the humility and simplicity of a farmer sowing seeds. The kingdom is hidden in humble form and comes into the world in seeming weakness. The message of the kingdom can be received or rejected. But for those who receive the word of God into a receptive and believing heart, the seed of the gospel will produce the harvest of the kingdom.

Second, Jesus teaches that the kingdom is already here, but not yet in its fullness. The parable of the mustard seed (Matt 13:31-32; Mark 4:30-32; Luke 13:18-19) suggests that God's kingdom is present among us like a growing plant. The tiny mustard seed grows to be the largest of plants, putting out large branches for all the birds of the sky to nest within it. So the kingdom is small and seems insignificant, but it is destined to be immense and valuable for all. Likewise, the parable of the yeast (Matt 13:33; Luke 12:20) teaches that the kingdom does not come all at once. Like the yeast in the dough that creates a powerful rising effect in the whole loaf, God's kingdom penetrates the world in slow but wondrous ways.

Third, Jesus shows in parables how the kingdom is not separate from this world. Jesus' disciples are rejected and imprisoned, and it seems that the forces that oppose them are more powerful than the message of the kingdom. When weeds are sown with the wheat and begin to spring up in the field, the workers want to root out the weeds immediately (Matt 13:24-30). But the owner instructs them to allow the wheat and weeds to grow together until harvest. Jesus teaches that the powers of evil and the kingdom of God exist together until God's final judgment.

Fourth, Jesus teaches that the kingdom requires us to be faithful and ready. Although many believed that God's judgment and wrath would fall swiftly on the faithless, many of the parables show that the judgment they expect does not fall immediately but is reserved for the end of time. Jesus offers the parable of the Ten Virgins (Matt 25:1-13), five of whom keep extra oil for their lamps and are ready to enter the wedding feast when the bridegroom comes. The parable of the Talents (Matt 25:14-30) shows how two servants invest their master's wealth and one does not. Upon their master's return, the two resourceful servants share their master's joy and the other is left in the darkness. The parable of the Division of the Sheep and Goats (Matt 25:31-34) demonstrates that those who care for those in need receive eternal life, while those who neglect the needy inherit eternal punishment.

Fifth, several parables demonstrate the patience of God in delaying the full expression of the kingdom until many more have entered it. In the parable of the Great Banquet (Luke 14:15-24), the host suspends the feast until the lost and forgotten ones can be invited to share in it. Likewise, the parables of the Lost Sheep, the Lost Coin, and the Lost Son (Luke 15:1-32) portray God's mercy in seeking out the lost and celebrating when they are found.

In all of these parables and in many more, Jesus teaches the true reality of God's kingdom, in contrast to the misunderstandings and false expectations of his listeners. When we begin to appreciate the reasons God hides the kingdom's glory and power, why the kingdom is concealed from many, and why God delays the kingdom's completion, we better understand our own place in the biblical story and our mission for the time between Jesus' proclamation of the kingdom and its full and final revelation.

 A **parable** is a saying or story that provides a descriptive metaphor for the "kingdom of God" or imparts a moral perspective. Only Mark and Matthew have parable chapters, large collections of Jesus' parables joined into one long discourse (see Mark 4 and Matt 13). Scholars agree that Jesus used parables as a special teaching technique, but most parables would have been spoken as individual sayings given at different times and in different settings.

Jesus Works Mighty Deeds

Jesus reveals the kingdom of God both in words and in deeds. As he announces the kingdom, God is actively at work establishing divine rule over the world. What Jesus teaches about the kingdom is concretely demonstrated by his mighty deeds. The kingdom is not just a timeless reality; Jesus shows its immediate, personal, and saving power.

In the first type of mighty deed that reveals the kingdom, Jesus casts out the spirit of evil through the Spirit of God. After Jesus heals a demoniac, he says, "If it is by the Spirit of God that I drive out demons, then the kingdom of God has come upon you" (Matt 12:28). Jesus' ministry launches an attack on evil in all its manifestations. The kingdom shows God's power in Jesus and by the Spirit to overturn the reign of evil in the world.

In a second type of mighty deed, Jesus cures sickness. Disease and its attendant suffering and ostracism are a type of bondage. Jesus' deeds of power over disease are unmistakable evidence of God's liberating power at work through him. When Jesus heals the blind, the lame, those mute and deaf, and lepers, people see God's renewing power flowing into the world to end the reign of sickness and pain.

When John the Baptist is imprisoned and begins to wonder whether Jesus really is the Messiah and if God's kingdom has come in him, he sends his followers to ask if Jesus is the one to come. Jesus tells them to report back to John that God's redemptive power is visibly at work.

> And [Jesus] said to them in reply, "Go and tell John what you have seen and heard: the blind regain their sight, the lame walk, lepers are cleansed, the deaf hear, the dead are raised, the poor have the good news proclaimed to them." (Luke 7:22)

The healing power of God's kingdom has come upon the earth. Surely he is indeed God's anointed king, the expected Messiah. His deeds of power demonstrate God's reign flowing into human history.

In a third kind of mighty deed, Jesus frees people from the power of sin through divine forgiveness. This seems to promote the strongest response from his opponents. When Jesus tells the paralytic "your sins are forgiven," the scribes declare, "He is blaspheming. Who but God alone can forgive sins?" (Mark 2:7). Although in this encounter Jesus forgives the individual sins of the man, the gospels make it clear that sin takes personal, communal, and corporate forms, corrupting all areas of life. The authority of Jesus challenges unjust social structures that relegate people to the peripheries of society, maintain poverty, and retain power through violence. Jesus confronts these distortions of human life by changing hearts and promoting reconciliation.

In another kind of mighty deed, Jesus restores people from death to life. When he raises Jairus's daughter, the widow's son, and Lazarus, we see the power of God's conquering even death. In bringing these back to life, Jesus demonstrates that death is not annihilation and that death no longer has ultimate control over life.

In a final kind of mighty deed, Jesus restores even the natural world from the distortions caused by sin. When Jesus calms the stormy sea, feeds the hungry crowd with a few loaves and fish, and directs an extraordinary catch of fish for tired fishermen, he demonstrates God's desire to restore the world to its original harmony. These local miracles are like windows through which we catch glimpses of a totally renewed creation.

The saving power of God's kingdom is directed against everything that opposes God's good and gracious reign over creation. Jesus reverses all the consequences of evil in the world: sin, guilt, demonic possession, disease, food scarcity, exploitation, abuse, and the powers of death.

Seeing the consequences of God's reign through these mighty deeds of Jesus, we may be tempted to wonder why Jesus didn't just cure all the sick and raise all the dead. Why didn't the Messiah solve all injustices and heal all the problems of the world? The answer becomes clearer at the end of Jesus' life and in the establishment of his church. Jesus has indeed established God's reign in the world and conquered the powers of sin and death. Yet, the full consequences of God's salvation of the world in Jesus continue to remain incomplete. It is that fullness toward which we work as his disciples and for which we hope in the fullness of God's plan for the new creation.

 The **miracle stories** (or **mighty deeds**) in the gospels generally share a familiar structure. Some thirty-five miracles are recorded in the gospels. Their form provides testimony to the oral tradition that helped to preserve them. There are often five parts to a miracle story:
(1) Description of a condition that needs healing
(2) Dialogue between Jesus and the one(s) needing to be healed

(3) The miracle effected through physical touch, prayer, or a gesture

(4) Testimony on the part of the one(s) healed, sometimes accompanied by Jesus' statement that the recipient's "faith" has effected the healing

(5) Reaction of bystanders and/or the one(s) healed

From the Scriptures of Israel to the Gospel of Jesus Christ

For Jesus and his disciples, the Scriptures are the books of the Torah, prophets, and writings, what Christians will later name the Old Testament. Soon however, the early Christians begin to produce their own writings, some of which are recognized by the church as inspired and come to be considered as part of the Scriptures. These inspired Christian writings begin to be read alongside the ancient writings of Israel in the church's worship.

These new writings are not simply commentaries or reflections on the ancient literature, nor do they replace or supersede the Jewish writings. They serve the community with their own distinct character, centered on the person of Jesus Christ.

The early Christians gradually come to perceive this new sacred literature as the New Testament, as distinct from the Old Testament. The Scriptures of Israel retain their own uniqueness and their own independent value. But something new and final has happened; the ancient Scriptures have been fulfilled and completed by the new event of salvation—the life, death, and resurrection of Jesus Christ. So now, as St. Augustine expressed it, "the New Testament lies hidden in the Old, and the Old Testament is made plain in the New" (*On the Spirit and the Letter* 15.27).

The Old and New Testaments are intimately united with one another because the God of Israel is the God and Father of Jesus. The old and the new form one divine plan of salvation for the whole world. Jesus, Mary, John the Baptist, and all the apostles are Jews, and the feasts and traditions of Israel form the setting of the life of Jesus and the early church. Both testaments are rooted in the themes and vocabulary of the Israelites, with quotations, references, and allusions from their ancient faith. Theological themes like covenant, salvation, faith, sacrifice, and forgiveness cannot be fully understood without a knowledge of both testaments. For Christians, the divine promises and Israel's hopes for salvation are fulfilled in Jesus Christ, yet both testaments look toward the same future, to the full manifestation of God's presence in the coming kingdom.

The early Christian community, guided by the Holy Spirit, realizes that the persons, events, and institutions of the Old Testament foreshadow the coming of Jesus Christ. Adam prefigures Christ; the promises made to Abraham and Sarah find their completion in the new covenant; the fullest exodus is the death and resurrection of Jesus; the ancient temple, priesthood, and sacrifices are fulfilled in the person and cross of Christ; and the psalms of Israel can be sung about him, through him, and with him. And the words of the prophets, as well as their suffering and martyrdom for justice, are brought to fruition in Jesus.

In the Acts of the Apostles, as Peter proclaims Jesus to the crowds in Jerusalem, he shows them how the children of the ancient covenant inherit the blessings promised by their ancestors. The coming of Jesus continues and completes the narrative of God's redemption of the world.

> Moreover, all the prophets who spoke, from Samuel and those afterwards, also announced these days. You are the children of the prophets and of the covenant that God made with your ancestors when he said to Abraham, "In your offspring all the families of the earth shall be blessed." (Acts 3:24-25)

The word "gospel" in the New Testament refers to the entire message and ministry of Jesus culminating in his passion, death, and resurrection. It is the "good news" of salvation to be believed, proclaimed, and lived. But as the decades advance for the early Christians, the oral proclamation of the gospel develops into a new literary form. This good news of Jesus becomes crystallized in the form of four unique portraits of Jesus, the gospels according to Matthew, Mark, Luke, and John.

Among the twenty-seven books of the New Testament literature, the four gospels are pre-eminent. They occupy a position in Christianity somewhat similar to the Torah or Pentateuch for Israel. The four gospels stand at the head of the New Testament as unique literary works that tell the story of Jesus from the perspective of the faith of the early Christian communities. And they are written to strengthen the faith of believers and help them know more fully who Jesus is and what his coming means.

Four Unique Portraits of Jesus

The four gospels developed gradually within the community of Jesus' followers. This process may be described as a series of stages from the coming of Jesus to the gathering of the four gospels into the New Testament.

The first stage includes the entire earthly life of Jesus. This first period includes roughly the first third of the first century. It includes his public ministry, his teaching and mighty works, and culminates in his death and resurrection. This is the good news, the original living gospel.

Through his preaching and teaching, Jesus brings people to an urgent awareness of God's presence and invites them to respond. He ministers to human need, healing the sick in body, mind, and spirit, by awakening faith in those who have lost hope. He teaches with a new authority and challenges people to rethink their entrenched ideas and attitudes. He calls people to repentance and conversion, and he assures them of forgiveness. When Jesus dies on the cross, his followers are disillusioned, but with the resurrection, defeat changes to victory. With the coming of the Holy Spirit upon the community of disciples, they begin to realize that the life, death, and resurrection of Jesus is God's great act of salvation. The Spirit enables them not only to remember the life of Jesus but also to understand its meaning for themselves and others.

The second stage comprises the oral proclamation and teaching of the good news of Jesus by his followers. This period begins with the death and resurrection of Jesus and continues through the middle portion of the first century. During this time, the disciples begin to spread the Gospel.

As they recall the words and deeds of Jesus, the tradition about Jesus begins to take on pattern and form. Every time a story about the life of Jesus is passed on through the spoken word, the speaker highlights its immediate relevance to the listeners by selecting, rearranging, simplifying, emphasizing, explaining, and dramatizing it. The disciples gradually formulate very effective methods for teaching his life and message as they apply his words to the lives of their audiences in various parts of the Roman world.

The third stage is the earliest writings of the Christian community. By mid-century, elements of the preaching, teaching, and worship of the early church begin to take written form. Collections of prayers, testimonies, hymns, professions of faith, passion narratives, and teaching summaries express the faith of the early Christians about Jesus Christ. These writings vary as they express the words of many different people, communities, periods of time, and points of view.

In the fourth stage, authors gather these oral and written traditions about Jesus to form four different gospels. In the gospels of Matthew, Mark, Luke, and John, we have the good news of Jesus Christ as witnessed by four different evangelists within the context of four different communities in four different parts of the Mediterranean world. Each author selects material from oral accounts and various writings, reducing and synthesizing some materials and expanding others with explanations according to the unique needs of the community being addressed. These four gospels took their final forms during the final third of the first century.

Each of these four portraits of Jesus helps us to see different aspects of who Jesus is for us. The words and deeds of Jesus' life vary from one gospel to another, and the events of his life are written in a different order in each gospel. Early attempts to harmonize the differences in these four and condense them into one version were strongly resisted by the early church. These four evangelists were primarily interested not in giving us a chronological biography of Jesus but, rather, in showing us who Jesus is and the meaning of his life.

The final stage is the formation of these four gospels into the canon or collection of the New Testament. By the mid-second century, the church recognizes that these four gospels express a unique and irreplaceable revelation from God. Even though other so-called gospels were written later, called apocryphal or "hidden" gospels, the four gospels of the New Testament form the earliest and most reliable narratives of Jesus and his significance for the world.

The earliest lists of New Testament books, from the last decades of the second century, include all of the major books of today's Bible. The gospels of Matthew, Mark, Luke, and John are listed first, followed by the Acts of the Apostles and the thirteen letters attributed to Paul. In addition, these lists include the letter of Jude, the first and second letters of John, Hebrews, the first letter of Peter, and Revelation. Only the letter of James, Second Peter, and Third John continue to be disputed for another

century or so. Through this gradual but steady process, the authoritative leadership of the church has selected twenty-seven books of the New Testament as its norm of faith.

The proclamation of the kingdom of God is the core of the good news brought by Jesus. This reign of God marks the completion of all the works and promises of God made known through the Scriptures of Israel. The teachings and mighty deeds of Jesus express the meaning and presence of God's kingdom as it is manifested in him. Gradually, the good news asserted by the early church becomes solidified into four distinct portraits of Jesus in the form of the written gospels.

In the chapters that follow, we will preview each of these gospels and discover the unique characteristics of each. We will also see how the gospel becomes incorporated into the letters and other writings that make up the New Testament. All of these writings were composed to be read in the context of the Christian community gathered for worship. So, like the disciples walking with Jesus to Emmaus, let us allow our hearts to catch flame as Jesus opens these Scriptures to us and speaks God's word to us along the way.

THE SYNOPTIC TRADITION

When we read the four gospels, we realize that in some ways they are similar to one another and in other ways they are different from

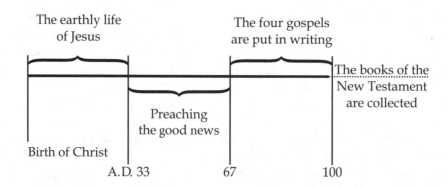

The earthly life of Jesus

The four gospels are put in writing

The books of the New Testament are collected

Preaching the good news

Birth of Christ

A.D. 33   67   100

one another. If these gospels were simply a recounting of all the events and teachings of Jesus' life, we would expect them to be almost identical. If, on the other hand, they were merely the interpretation of the life of Jesus by different people at different times, we would expect them to be very different. In fact, the gospels do both: they recount the words and deeds of Jesus, and they interpret those words and deeds in order to communicate their meaning.

So the gospels are both history and inspired interpretation. In light of the resurrection and the coming of the Spirit, the disciples of Jesus come to understand the meaning of his teachings, his life, and his death. The gospels certainly communicate information about the life of Jesus, but more importantly, they lead us into the experience of his life, death, and resurrection so that it can impact our lives.

allel columns. The reader can then see very clearly which words and phrases are the same and which are different from one gospel to another.

It should not be too surprising that there are differences from one gospel to another in the presentation of narratives or teachings. Jesus does not require a precise accounting of his deeds or a verbatim repetition of his teachings from his followers. He emphasizes, rather, a personal understanding of himself and his mission. For this reason, each gospel writer uses the oral and written traditions available in different ways. Under the inspiration of the Holy Spirit, the evangelists creatively structure and rewrite the material according to the unique purposes of each in order to meet the needs of their readers in different places in a variety of cultures.

Three Similar Gospels

As we study each gospel, we realize that the first three—Matthew, Mark, and Luke—are most similar to one another. These three are often called the "Synoptic Gospels," which means they have a common view. The reason for their similarities, and even word-for-word exactness in some parts, is due to the fact that they share sources in common. Most biblical scholars acknowledge that Mark's gospel was written first, and that Matthew and Luke use Mark's writing as the foundation of their works. This explains why nearly all the events contained in the Gospel of Mark are also contained in the gospels of Matthew and Luke.

Scholars also speculate that Matthew and Luke drew from another source—namely, a document containing sayings and teachings of Jesus. This source no longer exists, but the similarities of Matthew and Luke, apart from Mark's gospel, account for speculation about this lost source. To study the similarities and differences of these gospels more clearly, a reference book called a *Synopsis of the Gospels* or *Gospel Parallels* can be quite helpful. This handy tool shows each passage of the gospels in par-

The Composition of Each Gospel

There are three principles at work in the evangelists' composition of each gospel: selection, arrangement, and adaptation. First, each writer selects from the oral and written sources those narratives and teachings that best express the mission of Jesus and the purpose of his life. Examples of this selection on the part of the author can be seen in the following: only Matthew narrates Jesus giving the keys of the kingdom to Peter; only Mark recounts the healing of the blind man at Bethsaida; only Luke tells about the women disciples who minister to Jesus—and yet all the gospels narrate the miracle of the loaves and fishes. Each evangelist selects the parts of the tradition that best form his unique gospel.

Second, each writer arranges the material he receives differently. For example, Matthew gathers many of the teachings of Jesus and places them in the setting of Jesus' Sermon on the Mount. Mark describes the episodes of Jesus' life in a rapid-fire string of events that lead to his suffering on the cross. Luke forms many of Jesus' words and deeds into a travel narrative, marking his path from Galilee to

Jerusalem. In these ways, each evangelist shapes his narrative in a unique way.

Third, each writer adapts the material he receives according to his own particular purposes. An example of this adaptation can be seen in the gospel scene in which the crowds ask Jesus for a sign and Jesus responds with frustration in their inability to understand. Although this event is recorded in all the Synoptic Gospels, each writer adapts it differently. In Mark's gospel, Jesus states simply that no sign will be given, but in the gospels of Matthew and Luke, Jesus states that only the sign of Jonah will be given. However, Matthew and Luke interpret that sign differently from one another. For Matthew the sign of Jonah is the death of Jesus and his resurrection on the third day, while for Luke the sign of Jonah is the preaching of repentance by a prophet of God.

We see, then, that the selection, arrangement, and adaptation of the tradition by each author results in three very similar but unique gospels. Many of the so-called discrepancies in the gospels can be understood not as troublesome problems but as the result of the authors' artistic and theological use of the oral and written tradition. While faithfully transmitting the words and deeds of Jesus, the evangelists interpret his life so that we can understand and experience its richness.

Mark Announces the Gospel of Jesus Christ

For many centuries in the church, the Gospel of Mark was neglected and unappreciated among the four gospels. Since nearly every verse contained in Mark is also included in Matthew's gospel, a previous age thought it unnecessary to pay much attention to Mark. But in recent decades, there has been a rediscovery of Mark's literary genius. In fact, Mark is most probably the originator of the literary genre that we call "gospel."

Mark is a gifted writer in that he takes what was available to him from the oral and written tradition and writes a narrative that also contains his own insights into the meaning of Jesus' life. Mark gathers clusters of Jesus' sayings, collections of miracle stories, exorcism accounts, and compilations of parables, weaving them into a continuous narrative that culminates in the passion account of Jesus. His narrative of the life of Jesus is full of colorful, down-to-earth detail. More than any other gospel, he helps us appreciate the real humanity of Jesus by presenting his emotion, passion, and conviction.

Mark announces his gospel in the opening verse: "The beginning of the gospel of Jesus Christ, the Son of God." The Greek word *euangelion* is "gospel" in English, meaning "good news" or "glad tidings." Mark will communicate to his readers why it is such a wonderful thing that Jesus has come among us. The gospel will communicate the life of Jesus in such a way that it becomes good news for those who read it, enabling us to encounter him personally and experience his invitation to share his life.

Mark shows that the coming of Jesus Christ is both the continuation and the decisive culmination of God's saving plan for the world. He begins with a reference to Isaiah the prophet, yet these brief verses recall the entire book, especially the later parts of Isaiah in exile on which his gospel will be built. Mark is proclaiming that what Isaiah announces is now unfolding in its fullness. It is the news of comfort, the glad tidings that a way is being prepared in the wilderness for God's decisive return to his people.

> Comfort, give comfort to my people,
> says your God.
> Speak to the heart of Jerusalem, and proclaim to her
> that her service has ended,
> that her guilt is expiated,
> That she has received from the hand of the LORD
> double for all her sins.
>
> A voice proclaims:
> In the wilderness prepare the way of the LORD!
> Make straight in the wasteland a highway for our God!

Every valley shall be lifted up,
    every mountain and hill made low;
The rugged land shall be a plain,
    the rough country, a broad valley.
Then the glory of the LORD shall be revealed,
    and all flesh shall see it together;
    for the mouth of the LORD has spoken.
        (Isa 40:1-5)

The Jewish community at Qumran, the desert site associated with the Dead Sea Scrolls, understood its own mission as fulfilling these words of Isaiah. The discovery of the scrolls has led to speculation that John was for a time a member of the Qumran community. He preaches and baptizes in the wilderness near the Dead Sea, and becomes the one sent to "prepare the way" for the Messiah. As the last of Israel's prophets and dressed like Elijah, John challenges the people to look at their lives and prepare their hearts for Jesus Christ.

John's "baptism of repentance" offers God's forgiveness and is so attractive that the whole countryside and all Jerusalem come to him. The place of John's ministry, the wilderness and the Jordan River, evoke God's saving history with Israel. In the wilderness God prepared a people for the liberated life he offers them, and the Jordan River is the way through which God's people entered the Promised Land. John's baptism was a way for the Jews to reaffirm their identity as God's people—to come to the wilderness once more and to reenter the land of God's promises through the water.

When Jesus is baptized and comes up from the water of the Jordan, he sees the heavens being "torn open" as the Holy Spirit comes down upon him (Mark 1:10). Mark uses the same verb at the end of his gospel when describing the veil of the temple, torn open from top to bottom at the death of Jesus (Mark 15:38). This will complete the removal of the barrier between God and humanity—a removal that begins here at Jesus' baptism.

God is fulfilling the promises made through the prophet Isaiah: "The spirit of the LORD shall rest upon him" (Isa 11:2). The descent of the Spirit anoints Jesus for his ministry. Through the prophet, God's servant has spoken, "The spirit of the Lord GOD is upon me, because the LORD has anointed me" (Isa 61:1). God is bringing the expectations voiced in ancient times to their completion in the life of Jesus the Messiah.

Here is my servant whom I uphold,
    my chosen one with whom I am pleased.
Upon him I have put my spirit;
    he shall bring forth justice to the nations.
        (Isa 42:1)

Accompanying the descent of the Holy Spirit is the voice of the Father, addressing Jesus in words that echo Isaiah's prophecy: "You are my beloved Son; with you I am well pleased" (Mark 1:11). What Mark has said about Jesus in his opening proclamation—"the gospel of Jesus Christ, the [Son of God]" (Mark 1:1)—is now confirmed by God himself. Jesus is truly the Christ—which means "the Anointed One"—and he is God's Son.

However, Mark gives no indication that anyone but Jesus feels the Spirit descend or hears the divine voice. Jesus' exalted identity is hidden for now, though Mark's readers are privy to the mystery of this exchange between the Father, Son, and Holy Spirit. Readers might expect Jesus, as God's anointed Servant and Son, to reign triumphantly and vanquish the powers of evil. Yet, Jesus is driven by the Spirit into the wilderness for the final preparation for his mission. There he lives in a hostile environment with wild beasts for forty days and is tempted by Satan (Mark 1:13). The ministering angels who support Jesus in the desert recall the angel who guarded and guided the Israelites in the desert (Exod 23:20) and the angel who supplied nourishment to Elijah in that same desert (1 Kings 19:5-8). With his resolve tested, Jesus proves himself faithful in trial and ready for his messianic mission.

A Gospel Fashioned in Persecution

When Mark begins to write, the church has already expanded throughout the empire all the way to Rome. The magnificence of the imperial city at the height of its power disguises the terrible suffering of its Christian community. When the city of Rome burns in AD 64, Nero the emperor blames the Christians and unleashes a great persecution. Mark composes his gospel during this dreadful time.

Mark forms his portrait of Jesus amid the trials of the Roman church and the challenging questions of its members. Why is Jesus so powerfully attractive yet so violently opposed? If he has such power, why does he allow us to suffer so? How do we follow him while undergoing unbearable persecution? These are the questions in Mark's mind as he draws together the life of Jesus to hand it on to others.

Mark writes a fast-paced gospel that seems to be designed to create a sense of urgency. Jesus' ministry begins with the proclamation of God's reign now: "This is the time of fulfillment. The kingdom of God is at hand. Repent, and believe in the gospel" (Mark 1:15). The time for the completion of God's plans for the world is upon us. The message demands an urgent response.

Jesus moves quickly from place to place, taking the lead and determining the direction of the narrative. As the shortest of the four gospels, Mark's work lacks many of the lengthy teachings that fill the others.

The style and emphasis of Mark's gospel correspond to the situation of crisis in which it is written. The church in Rome is perplexed by its seeming failure and suffering, besieged with faintheartedness and fear. In this context, Mark writes a gospel that stresses the affliction of Jesus in which the entire narrative leads to the passion and cross. He wants to correct any notion that following Jesus leads to a triumphant life. He emphasizes that discipleship means self-denial, that following Jesus means taking up the cross.

The Structure of Mark's Gospel

Mark fashioned his gospel in order to enable his readers to answer two fundamental questions: Who is Jesus? and How do I follow him? The gospel is about understanding Jesus and understanding discipleship. Mark's gospel gradually reveals the identity of Jesus: through his preaching and teaching, through his miracles, and finally through his suffering and cross. And the gospel gradually teaches readers how to be disciples: through the good example of those called by Jesus to follow him and also through their many failures.

The gospel reaches its climax in the passion account. There Mark shows us that we cannot know who Jesus is unless we understand the necessity of the cross in his life, and we cannot know how to follow Jesus until we accept the necessity of the cross in our lives. If we are to understand the meaning of Jesus' life, we must see him as the suffering Messiah. If we are to truly be his disciples, we must know what it means to take up the cross and follow in his way.

The opening verse, in which Jesus is proclaimed with the titles Christ (*Messiah*) and Son of God, previews the whole gospel. These two titles must become for the church the response to the question Jesus asks midway: "Who do you say that I am?" (Mark 8:29). This is the central question Jesus asks his original disciples; it's the question that Mark's gospel asks of the early church; it is the question that all of us must answer for ourselves if we are to understand Jesus and follow in his way.

In the immediate response to the question, Peter answers Jesus, "You are the Messiah." Peter proclaims that Jesus is the anointed one, the one anticipated to fulfill the hopes of God's people. But Peter's response, while true, presents only a partial understanding of who Jesus is. It becomes clear quite quickly that Peter does not understand the role of the cross in Jesus' identity. The remainder of the gospel is spent teaching Peter, along with all of Mark's readers, a deeper comprehension of who Jesus is.

Throughout the second half of the gospel, Jesus instructs his disciples that he must suffer, die, and rise, providing them with a richer insight into his mission as the Messiah. Finally, toward the end of the gospel, as Jesus dies on the cross, the narrative climax is reached. The central question of the gospel, "Who is Jesus?" can be answered fully only at the cross. Ironically, the response comes from the lips of a Roman officer who sees the manner of his death. "Truly this man was the Son of God!" the soldier proclaimed (Mark 15:39), making the announcement that Jesus' disciples should have been there to make.

 Mark exhibits a curious feature that scholars have dubbed **"the messianic secret,"** or perhaps more accurately, "the secret of Jesus' identity." After many miracles, Jesus instructs the recipient(s) not to tell anyone; they abruptly ignore the command and spread the news of Jesus' miraculous ministry! This may be a literary technique to show how the characters in the story fail to comprehend fully the true goal of Jesus' ministry. He is destined to suffer and die on the cross for the sake of "ransoming" sinful humanity. Christian readers understand this meaning, but the centurion standing at the cross is the only human character in Mark to exclaim, "Truly this man was the Son of God!" (15:39). The "secret" is finally revealed (by a Gentile!) who watches Jesus' death.

Learning the Way of Discipleship

Mark's gospel shows how closely the two fundamental questions are related: Who is Jesus? and How do I follow him? An understanding of discipleship requires a clear and correct understanding of Jesus. The more a person is able to comprehend the meaning of Jesus' life, the more that person is able to grasp what it means to follow him as a disciple.

In the second half of the gospel, as Jesus begins to teach his disciples that he must suffer, die, and rise, he also teaches them about discipleship. Whenever Jesus predicts his own passion, his words are met with misunderstanding and resistance on the part of his dis-

ciples. Jesus responds each time by teaching them the intimate connection between who he is and what it means to follow him. This pattern is repeated three times as Jesus travels with his disciples from Galilee toward Jerusalem.

Following Jesus' first passion prediction, Peter rebukes him because he cannot accept the idea of a suffering Messiah. Jesus then teaches that whoever chooses to be disciples must deny themselves, take up the cross, and follow him (Mark 8:31-34). Following Jesus' second prediction of the passion, the disciples begin to argue over who is the greatest. Then Jesus teaches them that a disciple is to be the last of all and the servant of all (Mark 9:31-35). Following Jesus' third and final prediction of the passion, James and John request places of honor when Jesus enters his glory. But Jesus responds by dramatically reversing the way that power is exercised in the world and showing that the suffering Servant of Isaiah—the one who gives his life for others—is the model for both his life and his disciples (Mark 10:33-45).

In the account of Jesus' passion (Mark 14–15), Mark demonstrates the failures of the disciples most strikingly. The closest followers of Jesus fall asleep at Gethsemane as Jesus prays. Judas betrays Jesus with a kiss. The confident Peter denies Jesus three times. All his disciples leave him and flee at this darkest hour. No disciple stands at the foot of the cross in Mark's gospel. Every one of them has good intentions and a desire to follow Jesus to the end. Yet, they do not yet understand Jesus' continual teaching about the necessity of the cross.

Oddly enough the minor characters of the gospel respond best to the demands of discipleship. The blind man Bartimaeus follows Jesus to Jerusalem. The woman at Bethany anoints Jesus despite the protests of his disciples. The Gentile centurion at the cross proclaims the faith that the disciples should have understood. The women who followed Jesus from Galilee continue to minister to him in life and in death. A member of the Jewish council, Joseph of Arimathea, is the only one courageous enough to approach Pilate and give Jesus a proper burial.

Readers of Mark's gospel in every age readily identify with the disciples. They reflect the enthusiasm, misunderstandings, and failures characteristic of the church in Mark's community and of the church in every succeeding generation. Just as the grumbling and rebellion of the Israelites in the desert were written down for the instruction of each succeeding generation, so the incomprehension and failures of Jesus' disciples are written down for our instruction. When Jesus calls his disciples to follow him, he is calling us. When Jesus rebukes his disciples for their failure to understand, we stand convicted. When the disciples betray, deny, and abandon Jesus, we know that we have done the same. Yet, with the resurrection of Jesus, we are also offered his forgiveness and the hope of another chance to follow him.

The Unique Orientation of Matthew's Gospel

Matthew's description of a Christian scribe, as one who "brings from his storeroom both the new and the old" (Matt 13:52), may be an autobiographical statement of how he sees his role as a writer of the gospel. For more than any of the other evangelists, Matthew integrates both the life of Jesus (the new) and the Torah and prophets of Israel (the old). He presents references to God's word and work in the Old Testament and places them in relation to God's new word and work in Jesus Christ. This unique presentation of the old and the new makes Matthew's gospel the ideal first book of the New Testament. His presentation of the good news provides the entryway from the ancient covenant to the new, leading the believer from the history of Israel into the proclamation of the gospel to all the nations.

The way Matthew selects, arranges, and adapts the oral tradition and written material he receives to form his gospel can tell us something about the audience to whom he is writing. The gospel's Jewish perspective indicates that Matthew is a Jewish Christian, who writes within a community composed mostly, though not exclusively, of Jews who believe in Jesus. The frequent quotations from the Scriptures of Israel and the recurrent references to Jewish practices indicate a community concerned with the meaning of Jesus' life in the context of the tradition of Israel. This indicates that Matthew wrote to help Jewish Christians understand that their faith in Jesus is entirely consistent with their Jewish heritage. And, in fact, the messianic movement centered in Jesus is the most authentic way of living out the tradition of Israel in the later decades of the first century and beyond.

Matthew's gospel, like that of Mark, offers us a clear overture in the opening verse: "The book of the genealogy of Jesus Christ, the son of David, the son of Abraham." The word translated "genealogy" is the Greek word *genesis*, and may be also translated as "beginning" or "origin." It is quite possible that Matthew chose the word "genesis" for his gospel's opening verse to evoke associations with the first book of the Bible. As Genesis is about the origins of creation, humanity, and Israel, so Jesus is a new beginning for creation, humanity, and Israel. What God is doing in Jesus is a fresh, definitive, creative action for the sake of the world. All that God has planned and promised throughout the Scriptures is fulfilled in the coming of Jesus Christ.

Matthew's first verse offers us the most important titles or descriptors of Jesus' identity. Christ (*Messiah*), son of David, and son of Abraham—these three titles are the key to Matthew's expression of Jesus' identity. Each is an honored title within the tradition of Israel and links Jesus with Israel's history and with all the hopes of God's people.

Christos is the Greek word and *Messiah* is the Hebrew word. They both mean the "anointed" of God. Originally the word referred to one designated by God for a chosen role, such as a king, a priest, or a prophet. In later writings, Messiah is a royal title, designating a future ruler who will play a decisive role in fulfilling God's plan for Israel. Based on prophecies given to King David, the Messiah will free God's people from oppression and usher in a new age. Matthew's gospel will clarify what it means to call Jesus the Christ, the Messiah.

"Son of David" is a messianic title used frequently for Jesus throughout Matthew's gospel. It highlights the fact that the Messiah comes from the royal line of King David. He is a descendant of David to whom God has promised an everlasting reign. This Son of David will use his royal power to heal the needy and to bring about God's rule of justice upon his people. His messianic reign will be revealed not through force and conquest but through self-sacrificing love and service.

"Son of Abraham" links Jesus with the beginning of God's covenant with Israel, a covenant initiated with Abraham. He is the father of all believers, the head of Israel's royal lineage leading to David and to Jesus. The title portrays Jesus as the one who culminates God's plans that originated in Abraham. God has pledged to Abraham that his call and obedience will bring God's blessings to all the peoples and nations of the earth. What God accomplishes in Jesus as Son of Abraham fulfills that promise for the whole human race.

What follows in Matthew's first chapter is a theological genealogy that links the coming of the Messiah with the ancient history of the people of Israel. The long list of names, of both men and women, begins in the earliest history of God's covenant with his chosen people. This genealogy writes the fathers and mothers of Israel into the family tree of Christians. It demonstrates that the history of Jesus did not begin in Nazareth or Bethlehem, but with the stories of ancient patriarchs, prophets, kings, and generations of men and women leading up to "Joseph, the husband of Mary."

The Gospel of Christ's Church

Matthew's gospel, written after the destruction of Jerusalem and its temple in AD 70, reflects the growing tensions between Christian Judaism, represented by the community Matthew addresses in the gospel, and rabbinical Judaism, the emerging Judaism represented by the scribes and Pharisees. Both forms of Judaism claim to be the legitimate heir of the tradition of ancient Israel. This is a debate between two groups of Jews, not a conflict between Jesus and Jews, or between the Christian church and Judaism. Jesus and his disciples, as well as Matthew and the community to which he writes the gospel, are all Jews, seeking to be faithful to the tradition in which God has led them. When the Gospel of Matthew is read in later non-Jewish cultures, it can easily be misinterpreted as a Christian polemic against Jews, as history has sadly demonstrated. The reader of the gospel today, then, has the responsibility to consider the original context of the gospel, lest it fuel the kind of anti-Judaism that has so dreadfully distorted Christian history.

On the one hand, Matthew's gospel emphasizes the Jewish tradition of Jesus and his disciples, insisting on the continuity of Jesus with the Old Testament. On the other hand, the gospel is marked with debates and conflicts between Jesus and many of the Jewish leaders of his day. In light of this conflict between Christian Jews and rabbinical Jews, Matthew shows that Jesus and his divine mission are the culmination of the history of salvation manifested through ancient Israel. Jesus has completed the Torah and the prophets, inaugurated the long-awaited kingdom, and will lead his church to the end of the age.

The gospel shows great interest in the church, the organized community of disciples continuing the mission of Jesus in the world, and much of the gospel is concerned with teaching members of the church how life should be lived within the community. The church is not God's kingdom, but the kingdom is present in the church because of the abiding presence of the church's Lord. Jesus is with his church when the storm strikes on the waters, when his disciples are welcomed or rejected when preaching his kingdom, and wherever two or three are gathered in his name.

Because he is writing for the church, Matthew gathers the various teachings of Jesus into five blocks of teaching. These great discourses are the Sermon on the Mount (Matt 5–7), the sermon to the apostles (Matt 10), the sermon on the kingdom (Matt 13), the sermon on leadership (Matt 18), and the sermon on the last things (Matt 24–25). These five discourses have been compared to the five books that compose the Torah of Israel, and they seem to be designed to meet the catechetical needs of the growing church. Jesus instructs the church on how to live within the new covenant, to be humble, to seek out those who stray, to settle disputes, and to offer forgiveness. In this context, Jesus' fierce criticism of the religious leaders is not so much an attack on his Jewish opponents within Judaism as a warning to the future leaders of the church. The hypocrites and blind guides, who do not practice what they preach, who fail to offer mercy and refuse to listen to the prophets of their day, are not worthy to lead God's people. Unworthy leaders will leave the church as desolate as Jerusalem and its temple.

Peter's confession of Jesus' identity as it is preserved in Matthew 16:13-20 is important for Roman Catholic tradition. The church interprets this passage as the founding of the church by Jesus. This is the only one of the four gospels in which the word "church" (Greek, *ekklesia* = "assembly, those called") is used. The symbol of the keys given to Peter, the image of the rock as a firm foundation, and the promise that evil will never bring it down come together in a strong image of the church as the chosen people of God.

The Enduring Presence of Jesus with His Church

By presenting Jesus as the authoritative teacher of his church, Matthew's gospel helps Jewish Christians understand how to be loyal to the old covenant with Moses while engaging with new believers among the Gentiles. It confirms the continuity of the church with God's past promises to Israel while also validating the members' new loyalty to Jesus and his saving mission. As such, the gospel becomes an effective pastoral tool for the church's preaching, teaching, and worship.

To emphasize the divine presence of Jesus with his church, Matthew frames his entire gospel with this theme. In the first chapter, Jesus is called Emmanuel, which means "God is with us" (Matt 1:23). In the last verse of the gospel, the risen Jesus assures his community with the pledge, "And behold, I am with you always, until the end of the age" (Matt 28:20). As the people of the kingdom living in the new age of salvation, the church is able to live in the world with confident trust as it embodies the living presence of its risen Lord.

As the historical Jesus formed his disciples to be his church, the Jesus presented in Matthew's gospel forms the church throughout time to live as disciples in the time between the resurrection and his glorious return. In every period of Christian history, the Gospel of Matthew has brought direction and hope for Christ's disciples, inviting them into an ever-deeper relationship with Jesus, who promises to remain always with his church.

Despite the many similarities between the three Synoptic Gospels—Matthew, Mark, and Luke—each is written with a distinct purpose, to a particular group of Christians in different places and cultures. For this reason, they each recount the words and deeds of Jesus and they interpret those words and deeds in ways that communicate their meaning in differing contexts.

Because Jesus desires neither verbatim repetition of his teachings nor a precise accounting of his deeds but, rather, a personal understanding of himself and his mission, each gospel offers us a unique perspective. Each gospel offers us a portrait of Jesus in light of his resurrection and under the inspiration of the Holy Spirit.

In this chapter we have looked carefully at the uniqueness of the gospels of Matthew and Mark. In the next chapter we will examine the third of the Synoptic Gospels—the Gospel of Luke. Together these Synoptic Gospels give us three unique proclamations of the good news of Jesus Christ.

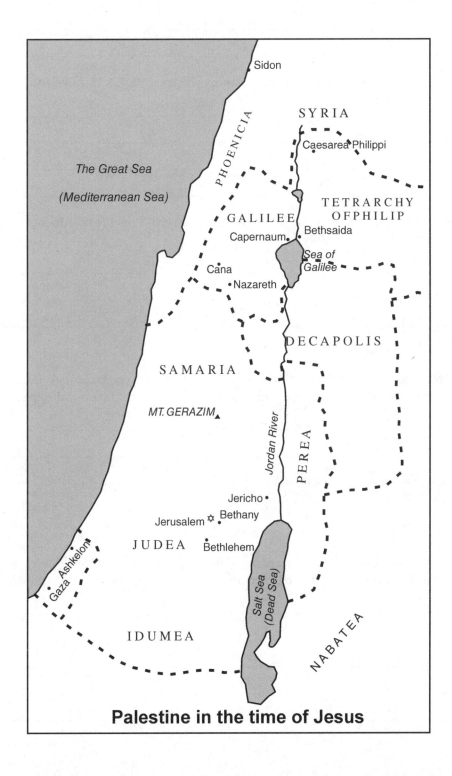

Palestine in the time of Jesus

EXPLORING LESSON ONE

1. a) What was the first century Jewish understanding of the kingdom of God?

_____

_____

_____

_____

   b) How is Jesus' ministry a fulfillment of this expectation (Mark 1:15; Luke 4:16-21; 7:22)?

_____

_____

_____

_____

   c) How would you explain to someone in your own words how the kingdom of God is both a present and a future reality?

_____

_____

_____

_____

2. A central message of Jesus' preaching is: "Repent, and believe in the gospel" (Mark 1:15). Briefly describe each key component of this message: *repentance, belief,* and *gospel*.

_____

_____

_____

_____

3. The commentary summarizes some of Jesus' parables about the nature of the kingdom of God. Of those mentioned in the commentary, which one resonates with you the most? Why?

_____

_____

_____

_____

_____

4. What are the five types of "mighty deeds" that we see in Jesus' ministry? How do these saving acts demonstrate the presence of God's kingdom?

_____

_____

_____

_____

5. How would you explain the relationship between the Old Testament and the New Testament? What value does the Old Testament have for you?

_____

_____

_____

_____

6. How would you describe the process of the formation of the four gospels, from the "living gospel" to the gathering of the gospels into the New Testament?

_____

_____

_____

_____

7. How is a gospel different than a chronological, historical biography? What does this difference tell us about how we should approach the gospels?

_____

_____

_____

_____

8. In Mark's Gospel, there is a clear relationship between Jesus' identity and the nature of discipleship. How does understanding who Jesus is help us to understand how we must follow him (Mark 8:31-34; 9:31-35; 10:33-45)?

_____

_____

_____

_____

9. After reading through the descriptions of Mark and Matthew in the commentary, what distinct traits of each do you recall, and what unique situations within their communities account for some of these differences?

_____

_____

_____

_____

CLOSING PRAYER

Prayer

"The Spirit of the Lord is upon me,
because he has anointed me
to bring glad tidings to the poor.
He has sent me to proclaim liberty to captives
and recovery of sight to the blind,
to let the oppressed go free,
and to proclaim a year acceptable to the Lord."
(Isa 61:1-2; read by Jesus in the synagogue in Nazareth in Luke 4:18-19)

Lord Jesus, in your ministry as God's anointed one, you proclaimed good news, healed the sick, raised the dead and forgave sins. As faithful disciples, may we also be signs of good news, healing, life and forgiveness in our homes and communities. We pray today for those in need of any type of healing, especially . . .

LESSON TWO

The Writings of Luke and John

Begin your personal study and group discussion with a simple and sincere prayer such as:

Prayer

Jesus Christ, you are the Word that reveals the Father. As we study the good news of your life, death, and resurrection, may what you reveal to us take root in our hearts and give life to our church and to our world.

Read pages 36–52, Lesson Two.

Respond to the questions on pages 53–54, Exploring Lesson Two.

The Closing Prayer on page 55 is for your personal use and may be used at the end of group discussion.

THE LUKAN WRITINGS

Following the writings of Mark and Matthew, Luke wrote the third Synoptic Gospel. Like the others, Luke composed a narrative of the events associated with the life of Jesus. But unlike the other evangelists, Luke extended the narrative of the gospel in order to narrate the life of the early church. Thus, he has created a two-volume work: the Gospel of Luke and the Acts of the Apostles. Together these two books comprise over one-fourth of the New Testament.

As a highly educated and polished writer, Luke demonstrates how the salvation promised to the people of Israel and accomplished by Jesus is extended to the Gentiles. He narrates the story of Jesus and of the early church not merely as a historical record, but in a way that enables his Gentile readers to enter the story themselves and discover it as their own good news. Writing with great detail and concreteness, he uses language that evokes the imagination of the readers and presents episodes from the life of Jesus and his church that become significant for the individual lives of his readers. Still, after two millennia, Luke's narratives show people how these stories transcend their settings in first-century Palestine to speak powerfully to people today.

Luke Introduces His Gospel and Acts

Luke addresses his two-volume work to a certain "Theophilus," a Gentile man of rank and a recent convert to Christianity. The shape of Luke's writings suggests that Theophilus is experiencing uncertainty about his place in a movement that was originally Jewish. Yet, Luke does not write just for one person. His writings speak to any non-Jew who feels out of place in the early church. Theophilus, whose name means "beloved of God," represents all Gentiles seeking to understand God's universal plan for salvation.

In an extended one-sentence prologue, Luke states that his gospel offers an accurate

history of the events associated with Jesus Christ. Since he is not himself one of the apostolic witnesses, but rather a second-generation Christian, he relies on the tradition that came from the apostles before him. He mentions his sources: the narratives written by others, accounts of eyewitnesses from the beginning, what ministers of the word have handed down, and his own accurate investigation. All of these elements contribute to a narrative that assures Theophilus and all of Luke's readers of the certainty of the teachings they have received (Luke 1:1-4).

When Luke moves on to his second volume, he summarizes the content of "the first book," the Gospel of Luke. "All that Jesus did and taught"—his choosing disciples, his suffering and resurrection appearances, his commission that his disciples be witnesses to the world, the promise of the Spirit, and his ascension into heaven—forms a transition to the new stage of history, the story of the church (Acts 1:1-5).

Through the Holy Spirit, God unites Jesus and his church. In the early pages of Luke's gospel, the Holy Spirit comes upon Mary in order to give birth to Jesus. The Spirit then animates and leads Jesus throughout the gospel's presentation of his saving ministry. In the early pages of Luke's second volume, the Holy Spirit comes upon Mary and the apostles to give birth to the church. The same Spirit then animates and leads the church through its foundational years as presented in Acts.

Luke demonstrates the unity and continuity between Jesus and his church by showing parallels between his gospel and Acts. The Spirit that comes to dwell in Jesus and empower him for ministry at his baptism also descends on the assembled community at Pentecost, dwelling in the disciples and empowering the church. As Jesus teaches and heals throughout the gospel, Peter and Paul do the same throughout Acts. As Jesus raised men and women from the dead, so do Peter and Paul in the raising of Tabitha and Eutychus. The trials of Jesus have their equivalence in the trial scenes of Stephen and Paul in Acts.

These many parallels are Luke's way of demonstrating that the life of Jesus continues in his church. As Jesus prays, preaches, teaches, heals, reconciles, and suffers, so his followers are shown doing the same thing. Luke's readers are invited into this ongoing account as disciples of Jesus, to do what he did, to be his living presence in the world. This ongoing narrative continues into the lives of all who receive the Spirit of Jesus and are ready to believe, pray, teach, serve, and forgive.

Salvation Offered for All People

Because of Luke's Gentile background and the needs of the community in which he writes, he creates a distinctive gospel focused on Jesus as the Savior of the whole world. The entire event of Jesus Christ, from his earthly ministry through the expansion of his ministry in the church, is framed by the theme of God's salvation. The life of Jesus is prefaced by the proclamation that "all flesh shall see the salvation of God" (Luke 3:6), and Acts concludes with the announcement that "this salvation of God has been sent to the Gentiles" (Acts 28:28).

Jesus was proclaimed as Savior by the angels at this birth, and both Peter and Paul announce that Jesus is Savior for Israel (Acts 5:31; 13:23). By applying this ancient title for God to Jesus himself, Luke assures us that God had brought salvation to the world in Jesus.

God's whole plan for the world can be described as the history of salvation. This divine plan has been revealed in the Old Testament, and the events recorded in Luke's gospel and Acts are the completion of God's ancient plan. Luke stresses the continuity of God's plan, which is worked out through three progressive stages.

The first is the period of Israel, from creation through the ministry of John the Baptist. The second is the period of Jesus, from the beginning of his public ministry to his ascension. The third is the period of the church, from Jesus' ascension to the end of human history. Through these stages, Luke demonstrates how God's salvation in Jesus Christ is destined to be experienced by all the nations of the world.

The first stage of God's plan is described by Luke as the period of the law and the prophets. In his writings this phase is represented by the beginning chapters of the gospel. Through the infancy narratives, Luke surrounds us with the faithful, hopeful people of Israel. His account of the conception and birth of John the Baptist and the conception and birth of Jesus assure us that the events to come are all rooted in Israel's past. The infancy stories and the ministry of John the Baptist show us quite clearly that salvation in Jesus is a development of God's ancient plan that has begun with all the people and events narrated in the Scriptures of Israel. Later in the gospel Jesus proclaims: "The law and the prophets lasted until John; but from then on the kingdom of God is proclaimed" (Luke 16:16).

The second stage is described by Luke in the main body of his gospel. It is the life, death, and resurrection of Jesus Christ. It is time for the fulfillment of God's promises. Luke begins the public ministry of Jesus in the synagogue on the sabbath day. In this inaugural scene, Jesus stands up to read and is handed a scroll of the prophet Isaiah. He unrolls the scroll and reads:

"The Spirit of the Lord is upon me,
   because he has anointed me
      to bring glad tidings to the poor.
He has sent me to proclaim liberty to captives
   and recovery of sight to the blind,
      to let the oppressed go free,
and to proclaim a year acceptable to the Lord."

Rolling up the scroll, he handed it back to the attendant and sat down, and the eyes of all in the synagogue looked intently at him. He said to them, "Today this scripture passage is fulfilled in your hearing." (Luke 4:18-21)

The "today" that Jesus proclaims marks the time in which the hopes and expectations of ancient Israel begin to be realized. It is the time of victory for the poor, the captive, the blind, and the oppressed. It is the time of salvation in Jesus.

The final stage of God's saving plan is described by Luke in the Acts of the Apostles. It narrates the history of the early church—as the message of salvation is proclaimed to people everywhere. Luke narrates the expansion of Christianity from Jerusalem to Rome, but the readers realize that the period of the church continues into their own time as they await the coming of the Lord.

Jesus is the center of God's plan to bring salvation to the world. He unites the past, present, and future. He is the one who was promised in the Scriptures of Israel and who brought salvation through his life, death, and resurrection. And it is Jesus who continues after his resurrection and ascension to offer salvation to all humanity through his representatives in the early church. Indeed, "there is no salvation through anyone else, nor is there any other name under heaven given to the human race by which we are to be saved" (Acts 4:12). The bestowal of God's Spirit on both Jews and Gentiles demonstrates that God treats everyone the same, gives the same opportunities to all, and calls upon all people to respond to the salvation he offers through Jesus Christ.

An Invitation without Boundaries

Luke's narrative convinces us that all people can come to Jesus and be included in his offer of salvation: the poor and the rich, the Gentiles and the Jews, women and men, foreigners and Israelites, the healthy and the sick, the sinners and the saints. Luke points out how Jesus associates with the outcasts, sinners, prostitutes, and tax collectors.

The mission of Jesus is stated in a variety of forms: "He has anointed me to bring glad tidings to the poor" (Luke 4:18); "I have not come to call the righteous to repentance but sinners" (Luke 5:32); "The Son of Man has come to seek and to save what was lost" (Luke 19:10). All who are in need—the poor, the sinners, the lost—can encounter a caring and compassionate God through Jesus. His message is one of mercy and hope. God's promises from the ancient Scriptures are fulfilled for all who turn to Jesus, reorient their lives, and trust in him. This salvation involves receiving forgiveness, experiencing God's kingdom, and being enlivened by the Holy Spirit. Such care and compassion know no boundaries of race, gender, ethnicity, or class.

Because of the way Jesus attracted those who are marginalized, he became known as the one who "welcomes sinners and eats with them" (Luke 15:2). Table fellowship is emphasized throughout Luke's gospel, and Jesus is depicted frequently as sharing meals with those on the fringes of society and peppering his teaching with references to food, banquets, and feasts. In the parable of the Great Banquet, expressing the inclusiveness and abundance of God's kingdom, the host sends his servants out into the city streets and back alleys of the town to invite the poor, disabled, and outcasts. When there is still room left at the table, he sends the servants out to the roads outside the town, encouraging everyone to attend from all directions (Luke 14:21-23).

In a series of three parables—the lost sheep, the lost coin, and the lost son—Jesus illustrates the joy in heaven over a single sinner who repents (Luke 15:1-32). The point of each story is that God will go to great efforts and rejoice with great joy to find and restore a sinner to himself. Through his teaching and example, Jesus shows his disciples that they must love people and draw them to God. They must reflect his concern and compassion, seeking out the lost and rejoicing over every repentant sinner.

Jesus' care for the outcasts reaches its climax at the cross. The one who has sought to save sinners and seek out the lost throughout his life now asks God's forgiveness for his torturers (Luke 23:34). Jesus dies between two criminals, breathing his last with the same kind of people with whom he has associated throughout his ministry. His words of mercy for his executioners seem to have inspired one of the criminals crucified with him to repent and place his faith in Jesus. The words of Jesus, "Amen, I say to you, today you will be with me in Paradise" (Luke 23:43), solemnly declare that he can and does save those who turn to him. This reconciled criminal is the final example and result of Jesus' mission to call sinners to repentance and to seek out and save the lost.

Hearing and Doing the Word of God

Luke is the only gospel to describe the preaching and teaching of Jesus as "the word of God" (Luke 5:1). Through the proclamation of the good news and the teachings of Jesus on the kingdom, God addresses his people. As the prophets spoke the word of God as recorded in the Scriptures of Israel, Jesus speaks so that people will hear the word of God.

Luke takes up the parable of the sower from Mark's gospel in which Jesus compares God's word to a seed. God sows the seed indiscriminately to all people, regardless of the condition of their lives. Those who hear the word must prepare the ground of their hearts to receive that word and allow it to take root, grow, and bear fruit (Luke 8:11-15).

Yet, Luke has already shown that Mary, the mother of Jesus, is the ideal woman of the word. Mary readily opened her heart to God's word in the annunciation God delivered to her:

"May it be done to me according to your word" (Luke 1:38). Throughout the infancy of Jesus, Mary continues to ponder God's word, keeping all these things, reflecting on them in her heart (see Luke 2:19, 51).

Immediately after Jesus explains the parable of the sower, his mother and brothers are seeking him. When Jesus is told, he says, "My mother and my brothers are those who hear the word of God and act on it" (Luke 8:21). Later, while Jesus is speaking, a woman from the crowd calls and says to Jesus, "Blessed is the womb that carried you and the breasts at which you nursed." And Jesus replies, "Rather, blessed are those who hear the word of God and observe it" (Luke 11:27-28). These are the family of Jesus, the children of the Father. Jesus wants to teach his disciples to listen to God's word and put it into action.

Luke invites all who listen to his gospel to hear the word of God and let it bear fruit. Mary is our first model for this faithful listening and responding. We follow her example when we reflect on the events of Jesus' life in our hearts. Our challenge as we read the narratives of Luke is to become disciples of Jesus by listening, reflecting, and doing the word of God today. Both Luke and Mary teach us to be contemplatives in action.

Luke also uses the phrase "the word of God" in the Acts of the Apostles to refer to the proclamation of the gospel by the early church. In this way, he links Jesus' preaching and teaching with that of the apostles. To be sure he describes the mission of the church itself as the expansion and growth of the word of God (Acts 6:7; 8:14; 11:1; 12:24; 19:20). So, the prophets of old spoke God's word through the Spirit of God, the same Holy Spirit anointed Jesus to speak the good news, and the Holy Spirit impels the apostolic church to spread the word of God.

In this same sense, the Torah and prophets of the Old Testament, the good news written by Luke and other evangelists, and the writings of the apostles and other ministers of the word in the New Testament are all inspired by the Holy Spirit to deliver the word of God to his people. Of all these sacred writings, we can truly acclaim, "The word of the Lord."

When these writings—"in the law of Moses and in the prophets and psalms" (Luke 24:44), and the gospels, the Acts of the Apostles, and the other New Testament writings—are proclaimed in the church's liturgy, we can be assured that the risen Lord will open our minds to understand the Scriptures, just as he opened the minds of his disciples in Jerusalem (Luke 24:45). We can also be confident that when we read the Scriptures in faith, we can expect our hearts to catch fire as we listen to God speak to us, just as the hearts of the disciples were burning within them as Jesus opened the Scriptures to them on the road to Emmaus. Our challenge now is to take away the obstacles that prevent God's word from flourishing in our lives and to become disciples by listening, understanding, praying, and doing the word of God today.

 Of the gospels, **Luke gives the most attention to Mary.** Artists throughout history have portrayed poignant scenes from Luke's infancy narrative (Luke 1–2) such as the annunciation and the visitation. Mary takes center stage throughout the story as it unfolds and her destiny to be the mother of Jesus is revealed. Mary expresses her response to God's mysterious will in the Canticle of Mary (Luke 1:46-55). Filled with Old Testament imagery, the canticle shows that Mary acquiesces totally to God's will, even without understanding it fully.

The Gospel and Acts of the Holy Spirit

Luke's gospel demonstrates that Jesus is filled with the Holy Spirit throughout his life, empowering him to pray, to teach, and to heal. After his baptism by John, the Holy Spirit descends upon him, and then Jesus, "filled with the holy Spirit," is led by the Spirit into the wilderness (Luke 4:1). In the first act of his pub-

lic ministry, Jesus declares that the words of the prophet are fulfilled: "The Spirit of the Lord is upon me" (Luke 4:18). Luke notes that Jesus "rejoiced in the holy Spirit" as he prayed to the Father (Luke 10:21).

The evangelist highlights the role of the Holy Spirit in Jesus' life because he wants to emphasize the Spirit's role in the life of his readers. Jesus promises that the Father will "give the holy Spirit to those who ask him" (Luke 11:13), and at the end of the gospel the risen Jesus instructs the apostles to wait in Jerusalem because he is sending upon them what the Father promised, the gift of the Holy Spirit to clothe them with power from on high (Luke 24:49). The Holy Spirit's guidance and empowerment in the life of Jesus sets the pattern for the Spirit's work in the lives of his followers.

In the Acts of the Apostles, the Holy Spirit animates the whole church in its evangelizing mission. In Acts, Luke mentions the Holy Spirit over fifty times, so much so that some have suggested that the book might be better entitled the Acts of the Holy Spirit. It is the Spirit of God who is the truest apostle—"the one who is sent" by God to empower and guide the early church. In his narrative, Luke traces the way the Spirit of God guides the community of disciples from the beginning of the church throughout the early stages of its growth.

Once the community of disciples receives the Spirit at Pentecost, it is able to act as Jesus did. The Spirit that was his alone is now poured out upon them all. Peter proclaims: "Exalted at the right hand of God, he received the promise of the holy Spirit from the Father and poured it forth, as you both see and hear" (Acts 2:33). From the time of Pentecost, all the major characters in Acts are driven by the Spirit to act courageously and preach boldly. Clearly Luke considers the Holy Spirit to be the "life-principle" of the church.

The Holy Spirit guides the mission of the early church according to God's designs. In what has been called a "triple Pentecost," Luke narrates the gift of the Spirit first to the Jews, then to the Samaritans, and finally to the Gentiles. In the first Pentecost, many Jewish people gather in Jerusalem and accept Peter's invitation to repent, be baptized, and receive the Holy Spirit (Acts 2:38). As Luke narrates the witness of Jesus' disciples expanding outwardly, he shows us that many Samaritans begin accepting the word of God. So the apostles send Peter and John to pray for the Spirit with the Samaritans, and they "laid hands on them and they received the holy Spirit" (Acts 8:17). The final expansion of the good news to the Gentiles begins in the city of Caesarea. While speaking to the crowd, Peter proclaims that "God shows no partiality" (Acts 10:34)—that people from any nation can experience God's salvation. As he was speaking, "the holy Spirit fell upon all who were listening to the word." The Jews who accompany Peter are amazed that "the gift of the holy Spirit should have been poured out on the Gentiles also" (Acts 10:44-45). This third "pentecostal" experience indicates that both Jews and Gentiles can be equally endowed with the gift of God's Spirit, thus making way for the expansion of the Christian mission to the whole world.

This same Holy Spirit, Luke wants us to understand, continues to direct the church, which had its origin at Pentecost and is now two thousand years old. As we read and reflect on Luke's gospel and Acts, we should be aware that the same Spirit who breathed in Luke as he wrote also lives today within the church and works within each of us as we read Luke's inspired books. God binds his own Spirit into these texts and meets us on the holy ground of these sacred pages.

From the beginning to the end of Acts, the **Holy Spirit** is a primary character. The Spirit is a sign of the guiding presence of God at work directing the life of the church. The Spirit emboldens the apostles at Pentecost and ensures the ultimate success of the mission of evangelization throughout the world. Later theology identified the giving of the Holy Spirit primarily with the sacrament of confirmation. Traditionally, seven "gifts" *(wisdom, understanding, counsel, fortitude, knowledge, piety, fear of the Lord)* and twelve "fruits" *(charity, joy, peace, patience, kindness, goodness, generosity, gentleness, faithfulness, modesty, self-control, chastity)* come with the reception of the Holy Spirit (see Isa 11:2-3; Gal 5:22-23).

The Journey of Jesus to Jerusalem

The journey is one of the central motifs in Luke's writings. As Luke describes Jesus traveling with his disciples, he invites his readers to accompany Jesus and to learn from him along the way. After Luke's narrative of Jesus in Galilee, he describes Jesus' journey to Jerusalem beginning with the declaration that Jesus "resolutely determined to journey to Jerusalem" (Luke 9:51). The city of Jesus' destiny is the goal of Jesus' trek, but the travel itself is important.

The journey is a time of training and formation. In ten chapters (Luke 9:51–19:27), Luke describes the teachings that Jesus offers his disciples as he prepares them to be his witnesses. Jesus clarifies the nature and demands of discipleship, a way that demands change and hardships. Jesus is coaching his disciples to be his church.

Most of the passages found uniquely in Luke's gospel are contained in this travel section. For example, through the marvelous parables of the Good Samaritan, the Rich Fool, the Barren Fig Tree, the Lost Coin, the Prodigal Son, the Shrewd Manager, and the Rich Man and Lazarus, Jesus forms the mind and hearts of his followers for the ways of God's kingdom. Only in Luke's gospel do we find Jesus' teachings on humility, on whom to invite for dinner, on seeking places of honor, and on the importance of counting the costs of discipleship. In this section, we find the story of Martha and Mary, which narrates the necessary dimensions of discipleship, and the description of Zacchaeus, who shows the only way a rich person can be a disciple. All of these passages set Luke apart from the other three gospels and demonstrate how Jesus guides his disciples toward the kind of personal discipline and conversion of heart necessary to become his witnesses in the world.

Following Jesus along the way, Luke's readers also travel into discipleship, learning what it means to follow Jesus and to participate in God's reign. Like the original disciples, we too must always be learning from Jesus and continually change as we take his words to heart and follow in his way. We know that our journey is the journey of the church. In fact, throughout the Acts of the Apostles, Luke describes the church as "the Way," another term for expressing the journey of discipleship. As his church, we travel with Jesus along the way, and like those disciples who were accompanied by the risen Lord on their journey to Emmaus, we know that we are accompanied by the Lord and guided by the Holy Spirit.

The Call to Evangelize the World

As Luke illustrates God's desire to bring salvation to all people by filling his gospel with people on the fringes, he demonstrates God's saving will in the Acts of the Apostles by demonstrating the worldwide mission of the church. In the gospel we see the lost, the sinners, the sick, and the outcasts brought into Jesus' inclusive mission, and in Acts we witness a further extension of that mission: to widows, centurions, merchants, jailers, philosophers, governors, kings, and sailors. The glad tidings of salvation reach through the entire range of humanity. Disciples of Jesus must be witnesses to every person throughout the world.

As Luke's gospel is structured by geography—Jesus' journey from Galilee to Jerusalem—so the Acts of the Apostles is also structured by geography. This map is set out for us in the commission that the risen Lord gives his disciples: "You will be my witnesses in Jerusalem, throughout Judea and Samaria, and to the ends of the earth" (Acts 1:8). The

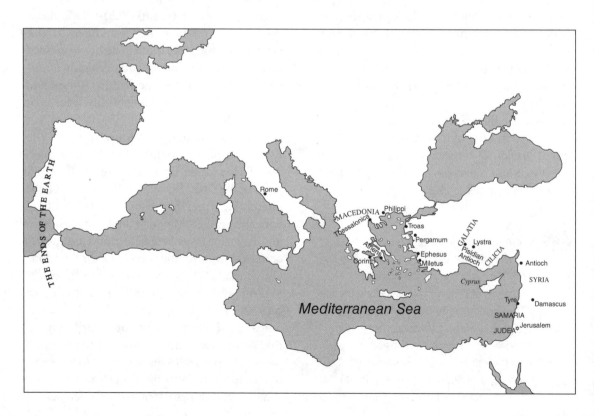

completion of God's saving promises is offered first to the Jews in Jerusalem, and then "to all those far off, whomever the Lord our God will call" (Acts 2:39).

Beyond Jerusalem, the good news is first spread to the Samaritans (Acts 8:4-13). Then the message of salvation is offered to an Ethiopian traveling to Judea (Acts 8:26-39). It is then brought to the coastal region, to the inhabitants of Lydda, Sharon, and Joppa (Acts 9:31-43). The outreach to the Gentiles begins with Peter's conversion of Cornelius and his household in Caesarea. The Gentile mission is then followed by the outreach to the Greeks in Syria, and then by the long journeys of Paul with his fellow missionaries. The journeys of Paul extend throughout Asia Minor, into Greece, and finally to the great and glistening capital of the empire, the city of Rome.

Jerusalem and Rome—a tale of two cities—the beginning and the end of the journey. While the church begins in Jerusalem—the heart of ancient Israel, the city of Jesus' passing into glory, and the city of Pentecost—it cannot rest there. Jesus has announced that Jerusalem and its temple will be destroyed. Impelled by the mission it has received, the church moves from Jerusalem to all the nations. There is no better symbol of all the nations than imperial Rome. Its Caesar is so powerful that he can order a census of the whole world, a call from Rome that set Mary and Joseph on their journey at the beginning of Luke's account. The call of Rome later sets Paul on the final journey of Luke's sequel. The Lukan narrative seems to reach its completion in the final chapter of Acts as it proclaims: "And thus we came to Rome" (Acts 28:14).

From Jerusalem to Rome, the people of God grow in number and devotion, accepting the gift of salvation that is offered to all. Those two cities, still today, stand as witnesses to the two-thousand-year-old proclamation of salvation in Jesus Christ. Yet, the writings of Luke are left unfinished and open ended. Although Rome seems to be "the ends of the earth" for Jesus' disciples in Jerusalem, we know that it is not the extent of the world's limits.

The ending of the Acts of the Apostles seems abrupt, leaving many details about the early church untold. But it feels quite unfinished because the goal of the work, witnessing to Jesus Christ to the ends of the earth, is incomplete. Luke wants his readers to feel the incompleteness of the narrative and then take up the story in their own lives and continue working toward the goal.

Where are the ends of the earth? From a first-century perspective, Rome is the center of the earth, not its end. For Jews, Greeks, and Romans, the world extends far beyond Rome: to Spain and Britain in the west, Scythia in the north, India in the east, and Ethiopia in the south. For twenty-first century disciples, the ends of the earth are wherever there are people who have not experienced God's saving love—it is all around us.

When Luke wrote his gospel, he knew that the story of Jesus was incomplete, and that it

Nearly one-third of Acts contains **speeches** proclaimed by the major characters (e.g., 3:12-26; 5:29-32; 7:2-53; etc.). Peter's Pentecost speech provides a stellar model (2:14-36). There is a loose pattern to the speeches that is repeated with some variation throughout Acts. The content of each speech is like a "mini-gospel" proclaimed to bring about conversions.

General Outline of the Speeches of Acts

- An appeal to be heard
- Scriptural background (Old Testament) to the message
- Proclamation of the significance of Jesus of Nazareth
- Further scriptural proofs of the message
- Offer of salvation and a call for conversion and repentance

must be continued in a second volume. The end of Luke's gospel pointed forward to the story of the church, which he wrote in the Acts of the Apostles. And when he wrote Acts, he knew that the story of the church was incomplete. The evangelizing mission of the church continues and demands a third volume. Yet, Luke does not write a trilogy; but he implies that it should be written. This third volume is an account that echoes the first two. It is a narrative similarly empowered and guided by the Holy Spirit. It is a story in which we live out the reality that despite the worst that can happen, God's word progresses, sets people free, transforms lives, and offers salvation.

Luke's gospel shows us the journey traveled by Jesus; Acts shows us the journey of the early church. Through this dual work of Luke we are invited to travel in the way of Jesus, on the journey of discipleship. The divine Spirit given to us in baptism leads our way, filling us with boldness and courage to continue the journey.

The road continues in the life of the church through time. Through our own discipleship we continue that "way" begun by Jesus and continued by Peter and Paul and a whole host of saints who have gone before us. All who read the pages of Luke's two books will know that they are called to be companions on the journey: Jews and Gentiles, rich and poor, men and women, sinners and saints.

As the early church formed the canon of the New Testament, Luke's two volumes were separated, and the Gospel of John was placed between them. The importance of placing the four gospels side by side took precedence over the importance of connecting Luke's double work. So it is to that fourth gospel, the Gospel of John, that we now turn.

THE JOHANNINE TRADITION

The Gospel of John shares many elements in common with the other three gospels. All four gospels narrate Jesus' inspiring words and powerful deeds as he traveled from Galilee to Jerusalem. They recount many similar stories, like the feeding of the crowds, the healing of blindness, and the events surrounding the crucifixion of Jesus. The four gospels draw from the memories and faith expressions of Jesus' early disciples as they recall his words and deeds, the power of his presence, and the impact of this experience on their lives.

Yet, the final words of John's gospel remind us that this account, like the other three, is only a limited view of Jesus, only a segment of his many words and deeds, only a fraction of all that could be said about him:

> There are also many other things that Jesus did, but if these were to be described individually, I do not think the whole world would contain the books that would be written. (John 21:25)

Although this fourth gospel bears a generic resemblance to the three Synoptic Gospels, it stands out as significantly different from the others. With its rich symbolism, its unique vocabulary, its developed theology, and its spiritual insight, John's gospel offers us a one-of-a-kind portrait of Jesus. In fact, 90 percent of the material of the other gospels is simply not found here.

John's gospel contains no description of Jesus' birth, no temptation in the wilderness, no calling of the twelve apostles, no transfiguration or agony in the garden. This gospel does not include the rapid accounts of miracles that fill the other gospels. There are no cures of lepers, exorcisms of demons, or stilling of storms on the sea. Jesus' characteristic teachings by way of parables, so common in the other gospels, are not found in John.

Instead, the Gospel of John presents a few choice sayings of Jesus for us to ponder: "I am the bread of life"; "I am the light of the world"; "I am the resurrection and the life." We find a few carefully chosen scenes that are highly developed for us to contemplate: the wedding at

Cana, the woman at the well, the raising of Lazarus, the appearance to Mary Magdalene.

The good news presented by John does not begin as the others, with Jesus' baptism or with infancy accounts. Rather, John takes us back before the world was created. The Word of God, who existed with God from all eternity and with whom God created the world, has now come to live among us as the revelation of God.

Revelation of the Unseen God

Although human beings have longed to encounter God throughout the ages in temples, rituals, and sacred writings, God is ultimately transcendent and beyond the human mind and senses. The Old Testament emphasizes this transcendence of God by stating in various ways that God cannot be seen by human beings. God says in the book of Exodus, "You cannot see my face, for no one can see me and live" (Exod 33:20). Yet, John's gospel proposes that humanity has reached a new experience in its attempt to encounter God. It announces that Jesus himself is the revelation of God, and that if we want to know the unseen God, we must look intently at Jesus. The last line of the gospel's prologue confirms, "No one has ever seen God. The only Son, God, who is at the Father's side, has revealed him" (John 1:18).

Jesus is the personal revelation of the unseen God. Because of the eternal bond of the Son with the Father, the life of God shines through the earthly life of Jesus. "The Father and I are one," he says (John 10:30). This oneness of the Father and the Son is not a fusion in which they are merely different disguises of the same person. Rather, the person of the Father and the person of the Son are joined in a perfect communion of love in which they are inseparably united and one. And this divine oneness and love between the Father and the Son becomes visible through all the words and works of Jesus. As Jesus proclaims at the end of his public life, "Whoever sees me sees the one who sent me" (John 12:45).

The incarnation of God in Jesus is the heart of the fourth gospel. The revelation brought by Jesus, the Son of God made flesh, makes possible a genuine and definitive knowledge of God. The Son is able to reveal God to us because he has lived with the Father throughout eternity. The Son has forever been "at the Father's side," an expression that suggests an intimate relationship that unites Jesus inseparably to the Father. And because the bond of the Father and the Son is one of intimate love, the revelation that Jesus offers us is not just one of doctrines about God but rather of letting the Father shine through his earthly life. As Jesus reveals himself, through the actions and teachings of his life among us, he shows us the Father.

John testifies that Jesus preexisted with God the Father who sent him down to earth for a time to testify to the truth and to bring people to faith. Then, in his passion, death, and resurrection, Jesus returned to his heavenly existence and glory. This descending-ascending movement is unique in the New Testament. Despite the "high Christology" (emphasis on the divinity of Christ) of John, the gospel retains a crucial balance, emphasizing both the human and the divine qualities of Jesus. Christian faith, as expressed in the Creeds, maintains that these **human and divine aspects of Jesus' identity** are equal: Jesus Christ is fully God and fully human. One aspect cannot overshadow the other without leading to a misunderstanding of the person of Jesus Christ.

The Completion of God's Story with Israel

The Gospel of John, like the Synoptics, interprets Jesus' words and deeds against the backdrop of the Old Testament narrative of Israel. In fact, the gospel shows the reader, in many convincing ways, that Jesus is the full and complete story of Israel. In Jesus, God is restoring his people from the exile their sins have caused and has come to dwell among them.

Beginning with the prologue of John's gospel, the evangelist describes the coming of Jesus using the language of Israel's wisdom literature. In the book of Proverbs, divine Wisdom speaks: "The LORD begot me, the beginning of his works, / the forerunner of his deeds of long ago. . . . / When he established the heavens, there was I. . . . / When he fixed the foundations of the earth, / then was I beside him as artisan" (Prov 8:22-30). These incomparable qualities of Wisdom are also praised in other wisdom literature. Wisdom is "a pure emanation of the glory of the Almighty"; "the reflection of eternal light"; "the spotless mirror of the power of God"; "the image of his goodness" (Wisdom 7:25-26). The tradition of personified wisdom in Israel emphasizes the presence of Wisdom with God at creation and Wisdom's search for a home among God's people.

In the gospel's prologue, John proclaims that Jesus is the true and full manifestation of divine Wisdom. He uses the Greek term *logos* (Word) to express this revelation of God's self in his Son. He is the preexistent emanation of God who comes into the world and dwells among us.

In the beginning was the Word,
  and the Word was with God,
  and the Word was God.
He was in the beginning with God.
All things came to be through him,
  and without him nothing came to be.
What came to be through him was life,
  and this life was the light of the human race;
the light shines in the darkness,
  and the darkness has not overcome it.

And the Word became flesh
  and made his dwelling among us,
  and we saw his glory,
  the glory as of the Father's only Son,
  full of grace and truth. (John 1:1-5, 14)

The term "in the beginning" echoes the opening of the Bible's first book (Gen 1:1). "The Word" conveys the idea of divine self-expression. The divine Word is God reaching out to creation, seeking to share divine being, revealing the nature of God as eternal love, forgiveness, and compassion.

Everything comes into being through the Word, which began to be known first through creation, then through the Torah and prophets of Israel, and finally through Jesus Christ. As God's self-expression, the Word encompasses Jesus' entire ministry, showing that all his words and works flow from his eternal existence and God's self-manifestation in salvation history.

In Jesus Christ, "the Word became flesh," the eternal Word has been born into frail humanity. In the incarnate Word, God "made his dwelling among us." Literally, God pitched his tent, taking up residence among his people in a way far closer than when God dwelt in the tabernacle of the wilderness or in the temple of Jerusalem. The Word became flesh ultimately so that we might share intimately in God's life, and John's gospel is an invitation to participate in his divine life.

These themes from the story of Israel run throughout the gospel. In the opening chapter, the gospel begins to develop the title of Jesus as "the Lamb of God, who takes away the sin of the world" (John 1:29). The Torah describes the sacrifice of lambs as a daily offering in the temple and as an atonement for sins. Likewise, the Servant of Israel's prophecies bears the sins and iniquities of others, offering himself "like a lamb led to slaughter" (Isa 53:7).

Jesus is presented in the gospel not just as any lamb but as "the" lamb, God's Lamb, the Lamb whom God has provided for sacrifice to take away the world's sins. The title anticipates the passion narrative in which Jesus is described as the fulfillment of the Passover lamb, which God commanded Israel to sacrifice as a memorial of their liberation from bondage (Exod 12). The Lamb will atone for sins through his sacrificial death, liberating people from the bondage of sin. The Lamb of God will take upon himself not only the sin of Israel, but "the sin of the world." But God's Lamb is not simply a victim; he is the Savior of the world. He is the one through whom God will forgive the sin of all humanity and reconcile the world to himself.

The temple of God is another archetype from the Old Testament that John's gospel develops. The glorious temple in Jerusalem is the primary manifestation of God's abiding presence with his people. But, like the prophets before him, Jesus demonstrates that the temple system is corrupt and in dire need of reform. His cleansing of the temple, early in John's gospel, not only challenges the temple system to make itself worthy of bearing the divine presence, but it also manifests his own identity. Jesus reveals that he himself will become the true temple by passing through destruction and being raised again: "Destroy this temple and in three days I will raise it up" (John 2:19).

The significance of these words becomes clear for the disciples after the death and resurrection of Jesus. The divine presence does not require a physical temple in Jerusalem, for the Word has become flesh in the world. The temple that will be destroyed and rebuilt in three days is Jesus himself, the new means of access to the unseen God, the new "temple" for the messianic age.

Another theme from the Torah developed by John's gospel is the manna in the wilderness. After Jesus feeds the hungry crowd, they remind him of the exodus:

> "Our ancestors ate manna in the desert, as it
> is written:
> 'He gave them bread from heaven to eat.'"
>
> So Jesus said to them, "Amen, amen, I say to you, it was not Moses who gave the bread from heaven; my Father gives you the true bread from heaven. For the bread of God is that which comes down from heaven and gives life to the world." (John 6:31-33)

The gift foreshadowed by the manna in the exodus event is completed in Jesus. The true bread is not manna from the sky, but the one who stands before them. Jesus does not merely give bread from heaven; he is that bread. The bread of life satisfies the world's deepest hunger. In contrast to material bread that perishes or even the "bread from heaven" given by God in the exodus, Jesus himself is the permanent food that gives everlasting life.

> "Your ancestors ate the manna in the desert, but they died; this is the bread that comes down from heaven so that one may eat it and not die. I am the living bread that came down from heaven; whoever eats this bread will live forever; and the bread that I will give is my flesh for the life of the world." (John 6:49-51)

Likewise, the theme of the bronze serpent in the desert is developed in the gospel as a foreshadowing of Jesus and his cross. During the wilderness journey of the Israelites, God commands Moses to craft a bronze serpent and mount it on a pole. Those who look at it will recover from the bites of venomous serpents (Num 21:9). Similarly, when Jesus is lifted up on the cross in glory, he brings healing to those who believe in him.

> "And just as Moses lifted up the serpent in the desert, so must the Son of Man be lifted up, so that everyone who believes in him may have eternal life."
>
> For God so loved the world that he gave his only Son, so that everyone who believes in him might not perish but might have eternal life. (John 3:14-16)

This ancient archetype from the old covenant prefigures the saving power of Jesus. The Israelites looked up at the bronze serpent in order to be restored to life; the one who believes in Jesus lifted up on the cross receives eternal life. In John's gospel, Jesus continues to refer to his being lifted up on the cross as both his crucifixion and his exaltation: "When I am lifted up from the earth, I will draw everyone to myself" (John 12:32). In his death on the cross is the power of his resurrection. When he is lifted up, he becomes the source of healing for all, drawing all people to himself with the gift of eternal life.

Seven Signs Lead Us to Encounter Jesus Christ

In the Scriptures a "sign" is an encounter with God that is intended to lead people to faith. In Exodus we are told that God multiplied signs through Moses, but the people refused to believe. In the book of Numbers, God asks, "How long will they not trust me, despite all the signs I have performed among them?" (Num 14:11). As in the texts of the Torah, John's gospel contains a series of seven "signs." Like the signs God worked through Moses, these signs in the gospel are works of revelation and encounter. They liberate people and lead them to salvation.

Rather than recount numerous miracles of Jesus as in the Synoptic Gospels, John carefully selects seven great wonders of Jesus and develops them into great dramas. These signs become powerful narratives in which the evangelist teaches about who Jesus is and the power of his saving presence in the world.

These seven signs, recounted in the first eleven chapters of the gospel, are the following:

Changing water into wine at Cana (2:1-11)

Healing the royal official's son (4:46-54)

Healing the paralyzed man at the pool (5:1-15)

Feeding the five thousand with the loaves and fish (6:1-15)

Walking on the water (6:16-21)

Healing the blind man (9:1-41)

Raising Lazarus from the dead (11:1-44)

These deeds of healing and power are significant in their ability to point beyond themselves. These seven signs each point to the truth about who Jesus is and the healing love of God manifested in him.

In each of these signs, the emphasis is placed on the meaning of the event and the deeper reality of the miracle. When Jesus cures a sick person, for example, the gospel makes it clear that this is a complete healing, a healing of the body and the spirit. When Jesus restores the sight of the blind man, the dialogue that follows makes it clear that Jesus has also given him spiritual sight in contrast to the blindness of the Pharisees. When Jesus gives physical life to Lazarus, it is an outward manifestation of the eternal life Jesus gives to all. Physical health, sight, and life are gifts that anticipate God's total healing, true vision, and eternal life. These gifts that Jesus offers are manifestations of the life that God wants to give to all people as they encounter him through the life of his Son.

Tragically, as was the experience of Moses during the exodus, many did not come to faith in Jesus despite the many signs. At the end of the seven signs, the gospel notes, "Although he had performed so many signs in their presence they did not believe in him" (12:37). The challenge for the readers of John's gospel is to allow the seven signs to lead them to a transforming encounter with Jesus. Toward the end of the gospel, Jesus clearly states the purpose of the signs:

> Now Jesus did many other signs in the presence of [his] disciples that are not written in this book. But these are written that you may come to believe that Jesus is the Messiah, the Son of God, and that through this belief you may have life in his name. (John 20:30-31)

Although Jesus worked many other signs, the ones included in this gospel are presented as convincing evidence that Jesus is the Messiah and Son of God. Believing on account of these signs, which culminate in the great sign of Jesus lifted up on the cross, leads to life in his name. This life, which begins now and lasts forever, is John's wish for those who read this gospel.

Jesus as Fully Human and Truly Divine

John's gospel stresses the dual nature of Jesus as both human and divine. His two natures do not compete with one another, but both manifest the full reality of the incarnation.

Truly the Word has become flesh and dwelt among us.

Jesus' humanity is unmistakable. The gospel shows us that Jesus experiences the weariness of a tired body and the powerful emotions of the human heart. John shows him as angry in the temple courts, tired as he sits down at the well in Samaria, visibly weeping at the death of his friend Lazarus, and crying out on the cross with parched lips, "I thirst."

The gospel sets this very human Jesus in a truly physical world. John's writing indicates a detailed knowledge of the geography of Palestine, its regions and peoples. The author writes in amazingly accurate detail about the city of Jerusalem: for example, the sheep gate and the pool of Bethesda, the pool of Siloam, Solomon's portico, the stone pavement of Pilate's praetorium, and Golgotha, which he says looks like a skull. Much of the gospel reads like that of an eyewitness, giving us many extra details that enhance our experience of Jesus living within the historical reality of his times.

Yet, at the same time, John's gospel offers us an explicit emphasis on the divine nature of Jesus. This is achieved more effectively in those passages in which Jesus identifies himself with the name of God from the Old Testament. In the book of Exodus, God reveals himself to Moses as "I am who I am," and God instructs Moses to tell the Israelites, "I AM has sent me to you" (Exod 3:14). When Jesus refers to himself as "I AM," anyone who knows the Old Testament will immediately recall God's encounter with Moses at the burning bush, a designation emphasizing the uniqueness and majesty of God.

During the Feast of Booths (also known as Tabernacles), commemorating the journey of the Israelites in the desert, Jesus addresses the crowds saying that he will lead his followers into the fullness of freedom and life. During the exodus, God's people would have died in the desert if they had not been led by the God revealed to them as I AM. Now Jesus proclaims that he is that saving presence for God's people: "If you do not believe that I AM, you will die in your sins" (John 8:24). And Jesus announces that the fullness of his saving presence will be revealed in his future glorification on the cross: "When you lift up the Son of Man, then you will realize that I AM" (8:28). Jesus continues to explain that even Abraham looked forward to this day when all peoples would be blessed through Abraham's offspring. Jesus speaks with the voice of the God of Abraham, Isaac, and Jacob, the God of the living: "Amen, amen, I say to you, before Abraham came to be, I AM" (John 8:58). But this solemn claim to divinity is too much for the crowd, and they took up stones to throw at this blasphemer.

As Jesus enters his passion, he washes the feet of his disciples and then declares that one of those at the table will betray him. He explains the reason for announcing his knowledge of his betrayer: "I am telling you before it happens, so that when it happens you may believe that I AM" (13:19). Then, at his arrest in the garden, Jesus goes out and says to those who have come to arrest him, "Whom are you looking for?" They answer him, "Jesus the Nazorean." And Jesus says to them, "I AM." When he says to them, "I AM," they turn away and fall to the ground (John 18:4-6). The forces opposed to Jesus are powerless when confronted with the power of God.

Through this divine title and in many other ways throughout the gospel, John presents Jesus as divine, sharing in the nature of God. At other places throughout the gospel, the bold statement, I AM, is accompanied by images that describe aspects of the mission Jesus has received from his Father. There are seven instances of these solemn titles of Jesus.

"I am the bread of life." (John 6:35)

"I am the light of the world." (John 8:12)

"I am the gate for the sheep." (John 10:7)

"I am the good shepherd." (John 10:11)

"I am the resurrection and the life." (John 10:25)

"I am the way and the truth and the life." (John 14:6)

"I am the true vine." (John 15:1)

These seven descriptors are keys to understanding the nature of Jesus and his work in the world. The titles describe who Jesus is in relationship to us. Each is a statement about Jesus to contemplate. By reflecting on these divine titles of Jesus, we can be drawn into a deeper appreciation of him and trust in the salvation he offers.

The Gospel Call to Believe and to Love

The Gospel of John is an invitation for the reader to enter into intimacy with God through Jesus Christ. We respond to that invitation in two closely connected ways: believing and loving. These two responses are the foundation of the Christian way of life. The first letter of John sums up this dual response to God. "And his commandment is this: we should believe in the name of his Son, Jesus Christ, and love one another just as he commanded us." All who believe in him and love one another "remain in him, and he in them," resulting in an unimaginable closeness with God (1 John 3:23-24).

Believing and loving are inseparable. True believing always leads to genuine loving. These human responses to God's revelation in Jesus are most often expressed as active verbs in John's gospel. The verb "believe" is found over ninety times in the gospel, primarily in its first part. The verb "love" occurs more predominantly in the second part. The general movement throughout the gospel is from faith to love, from believing to loving.

In John's gospel believing is not just an intellectual ascent to particular truths, but rather a personal attachment and commitment to Jesus. It is the acceptance of Jesus as the personal revelation of God. Believing joins a person to Jesus in a way that involves the person's whole existence. Because it is a dynamic reality, believing implies a process of growth, complete with crises of faith and periods of trial. It includes elements of trust, commitment, fidelity, and witness.

Jesus never imposes belief, and the ability to believe is ultimately a gift from God. It is freely offered; each individual must freely respond. The disciples of Jesus hesitate, fluctuate, and falter. But eventually they come to accept him personally and to believe in him fully, like Thomas, to whom Jesus said, "Do not be unbelieving, but believe," and who said to Jesus, "My Lord and my God!" (John 20:27-28). The result of believing in Jesus is intimacy of life with God forever, "for God so loved the world that he gave his only Son, so that everyone who believes in him might not perish but might have eternal life" (John 3:16).

For those who accept the invitation to believe in him, Jesus gives them only one instruction: "I give you a new commandment: love one another. As I have loved you, so you also should love one another" (John 13:34). The command to love is not new, but it is the quality of that love that Jesus makes new. The disciples must love one another as Jesus has loved them. The love that inspires and empowers love of others is the love revealed in the life, and especially in the death, of Jesus. This quality of love leads to the giving of the lover's life: "No one has greater love than this, to lay down one's life for one's friends" (15:13). This love impels us to continually give ourselves, placing ourselves in the service of others. To give one's live is an abiding characteristic of Christian love.

Jesus tells his disciples that believing in him and loving one another will enable them to continue his mission in the world. When Jesus returns to the Father, believers will do the work of Jesus to an even greater extent than Jesus did during his earthly life. In his parting address, he offers this wonderful assurance: "Whoever believes in me will do the works that I do, and will do greater ones than these" (John 14:12). The internal life of the Christian community flows out to the world: "This is how all will know that you are my disciples, if you have love for one another" (13:35). By the demonstration of his life-giving love, the world will recognize the disciples of Jesus and be drawn to the animating love of Christian community. When disciples believe and love, Jesus, his Spirit, and the Father are present, and the disciples form a community unlike any other.

Reading the Gospel of John may sometimes seem difficult, but truly it is our easier task. The bigger challenge comes in putting it into practice. But we know that we can fulfill the instructions of Jesus in the gospel because we have been brought into a life far beyond our imagining. Through Jesus, the Word of God, we are able to know the unseen God and be drawn into the love of the Father. Through Jesus, the way, the truth, and the life, we may share intimately in the life of our God.

 John's gospel never reveals the identity of the **Beloved Disciple.** Ancient tradition identifies him with John, son of Zebedee, and presumed author of the gospel. Regardless of the accuracy of this identification, the "one whom Jesus loved" was an important authority in the Johannine community and the source of authentic witness for the gospel. He also provides a model for readers, since he is the one who regularly comes to faith and understanding prior to the other disciples of Jesus, including Peter.

Three Letters of John in Relationship to the Gospel

The three letters of John, commonly called First, Second, and Third John, focus on some of the same themes as the gospel. They were probably written after the gospel, attempting to encourage a correct interpretation of the gospel within the Johannine community.

It seems that some of the strengths of John's spirituality have become weaknesses in his community because they have been carried to an extreme. The gospel emphasizes the divine nature of Jesus, for example, but some in the community seem to be ignoring the physical humanity of Jesus. The gospel highlights the role of the Spirit as the source of authority, but now some in the community are refusing to submit to the human authorities in the church. So these very positive themes of the gospel

have become distorted because they have become unbalanced. The apostolic church of John's community is shown to be undergoing a process that the church must continually experience—balancing extremes and redirecting the vision.

The prologue of John's first letter offers a striking parallel to the prologue of the gospel. The writer roots the message in the historical, tangible experience of Jesus Christ, the incarnate Word.

> What was from the beginning,
>> what we have heard,
>> what we have seen with our eyes,
>> what we looked upon
>> and touched with our hands
>> concerns the Word of life—
> for the life was made visible;
>> we have seen it and testify to it
>> and proclaim to you the eternal life
>> that was with the Father and was made
>>> visible to us—
> what we have seen and heard
>> we proclaim now to you,
>> so that you too may have fellowship with us;
>> for our fellowship is with the Father
>> and with his Son, Jesus Christ. (1 John 1:1-3)

There are three major themes that seem to dominate both the gospel and the letters of John—they are light, life, and love. Together, these three great themes form the pattern of our deepening experience of Christ.

In this age of electricity, it is hard for us to imagine the importance of light in the ancient world. But the Scriptures use light abundantly as an image of God. The prophets of the Old Testament proclaim that the world is shadowed by the darkness of ignorance and sin and that it awaits the dawning light of the Messiah. In the gospel, after proclaiming himself as the light of the world, Jesus encourages his followers: "While you have the light, believe in the light, so that you may become children of the light" (John 12:36) The first letter proclaims that God is light and in him there is no darkness; therefore, "If we walk in the light as he is in the light, then we have fellowship with one another" (1 John 1:7). The light is the truth and goodness of God made known in Jesus Christ. We are urged to live in that light and to radiate that light to others in the midst of a world that is still sitting in darkness.

The very purpose of John's gospel is to proclaim the life that God wants to give us in Jesus Christ. The deepest human instinct and longing is for life. Death does not make sense, because every fiber of our being proclaims that we were made for life. All the signs that Jesus performs and all the teachings he gives have a single purpose: that we may have life. In the gospel Jesus summarized his coming among us in this way: "I came so that they might have life and have it more abundantly" (John 10:10). In John's first letter we find the same summary of the life of Christ: "This is the promise that he made us: eternal life" (1 John 2:25). This eternal life is not just life after death; it is a new kind of life here and now. The life of Christ within us is eternal life, which has already begun for us. Whoever lives and believes in Christ will never truly die.

The very heart of the Johannine writings is love. The incarnate Son of God says and does everything out of love for the Father, and he directs his disciples to do the same. In the Last Supper discourse, Jesus says, "Whoever loves me will be loved by my Father, and I will love him and reveal myself to him" (John 14:21). Indeed, in John's letters, after God is described as light and life, God is described as love itself:

"God is love, and whoever remains in love remains in God and God in him" (1 John 4:16). The greatest sign of God's love for us, John tells us, is that Christ laid down his life for us. Because we have experienced such love, we ought to love one another with this kind of love.

John's writings invite us to grow in our relationship with Christ. When we reflect on these themes of light, life, and love, we understand that they are the pathway for the Christian experience of God through Jesus Christ. We first encounter Christ as the light of truth, as the revelation of God in our midst. Then we experience his life within us, through the work of his Spirit, through the waters of life and the bread of life. Finally, our relationship with Christ grows in love. A love that we experience through his saving and sacrificial love for us, a love that we are challenged to offer as we give our lives for others.

Each of the four gospels forms us as disciples by offering us new ways to know, love, and serve God through following Jesus. Likewise, the many letters of the New Testament offer us new perspectives on the Christian life. Like the three letters of John, the letters of Paul and others present us with distinctive ways to understand Jesus Christ and to join our lives to his. We turn next to this wide display of letters that the New Testament offers.

EXPLORING LESSON TWO

1. a) What are the three stages in God's plan of salvation in human history, according to Luke and Acts?

_____

_____

_____

   b) What does it mean to you to think of yourself and your faith community as part of the third stage of God's plan?

_____

_____

_____

2. How would you describe the inclusive nature of Jesus' mission in Luke's gospel? What is Jesus' attitude toward sinners (Luke 5:32; 15:2; 19:10)?

_____

_____

_____

_____

3. In Luke's gospel, Jesus says, "My mother and my brothers are those who hear the word of God and act on it" (8:21). What does this mean to you? How do you value prayer and action, and how do they work together in your life?

_____

_____

_____

_____

4. a) What is the role of the Holy Spirit in Luke and Acts (Luke 4:1, 18; Acts 1:8; 4:8; 20:22)?

_____

_____

_____

   b) How do you see the Spirit at work in your life and in the church?

_____

_____

_____

5. A long section of Luke's gospel is known as the "travel section" or the "journey narrative" (9:51–19:27). In this section, Jesus teaches about discipleship, and those who journey with Jesus learn more about him. In what way is your life a spiritual journey? Where did you come from? Where are you going? What have you learned?

_____

_____

_____

_____

6. In his prologue, John writes, "No one has ever seen God. The only Son, God, who is at the Father's side, has revealed him" (John 1:18). According to John's gospel, why is Jesus able to fully reveal the Father?

_____

_____

_____

_____

7. Seven signs in the Gospel of John "point to the truth about who Jesus is and the healing love of God manifested in him." Which of these signs speaks most clearly to your heart at this time, revealing Jesus to you and increasing your faith in him? (See John 2:1-11; 4:46-54; 5:1-15; 6:1-15; 6:16-21; 9:1-41; 11:1-44.)

_____

_____

_____

_____

8. What are some of the ways that John emphasizes both the humanity and the divinity of Jesus? (See, for example, John 1:1-3, 14; 8:58; 10:30; 11:35.)

_____

_____

_____

9. "This is how all will know that you are my disciples, if you have love for one another" (John 13:35; see also 1 John 4:7-21). How well do you think we as a church are doing in bearing witness to the love Jesus asks of us? Can we be readily identified as his disciples?

_____

_____

_____

_____

CLOSING PRAYER

Prayer

"I am the resurrection and the life; whoever believes in me, even if he dies, will live, and everyone who lives and believes in me will never die. Do you believe this?"
(John 11:25-26)

Yes, Lord Jesus, we believe that you are the resurrection and the life. Through your life, death and resurrection, you have fully revealed God to us as love. May our lives always bear witness to you as we follow your clear and simple command to "love one another." Today we pray for those who are most in need of your love and ours, especially . . .

LESSON THREE

The Pauline Letters

Begin your personal study and group discussion with a simple and sincere prayer such as:

Prayer

Jesus Christ, you are the Word that reveals the Father. As we study the good news of your life, death, and resurrection, may what you reveal to us take root in our hearts and give life to our church and to our world.

Read pages 58–73, Lesson Three.

Respond to the questions on pages 74–75, Exploring Lesson Three.

The Closing Prayer on page 76 is for your personal use and may be used at the end of group discussion.

THE GREAT LETTERS OF PAUL

There are thirteen letters in the New Testament attributed to Paul, and some of these are the earliest writings of the New Testament. Paul is a master of words; he expresses himself personally, passionately, and insightfully. He has a fiery temperament and is able to argue forcefully. He can also forgive mercifully and speak about faith, hope, and love in beautiful language. He has a sharp mind and possesses the unique ability to express the most essential elements of the Christian faith in a language understandable to everyone. Most of all, he deeply loves Jesus Christ and dedicates his life to proclaiming the good news of salvation in him.

The early church looked upon Paul as the hero of the church's expanding mission. He fits his writing in between traveling, preaching, pastoral care, and working for a living as a tentmaker. His letters are not always developed theological essays because they are written to meet specific needs in various communities at different times. Sometimes they may seem disconnected because we have only one side of the correspondence. We don't always know the specific problems or questions to which he is responding. But his writings are always powerful, profound, and inspiring. They have come down to us in the New Testament as a collection of some of the church's earliest reflections on the implications of faith in Jesus Christ.

Paul's Experience of Call and Conversion

At the root of Paul's missionary travels and many writings is his extraordinary experience of conversion, his unexpected change of commitment, values, and identity. He had begun to violently persecute the followers of Jesus. With fanatic zeal he tried to destroy the church. But God turns his plans upside down and his life inside out.

The heart of Paul's experience of conversion is God's choice to reveal his Son to him. The account is told three times in the Acts of the Apostles, and Paul refers to it in his letters. But like any genuine experience of God's revelation, it cannot be adequately expressed in words.

The experience is narrated in a form similar to the Old Testament calls of Abraham, Jacob, and Moses. Paul journeys toward Damascus. He sees a great light from heaven, and he hears a voice speaking to him. Like the prophets of Israel, Paul knows that he was set apart by God before he was born and called through God's grace to be an apostle of Jesus Christ. His vision has been changed, the scale of his values reversed.

The result of his experience is a deepened understanding of God. He now knows that Jesus Christ is the means whereby people are put in right relationship with God. Now he knows that salvation comes in Jesus Christ—in knowing him and living in him. His new understanding of Christ's death and resurrection fills him with an irresistible compulsion to proclaim that good news to the world.

All of his writings, then, are an elaboration of his experience of conversion. This new revelation brought with it conflict and tension. But in the midst of controversy Paul comes to understand the truth of Christ more fully. And in tension he learns how to express it and apply it to the variety of circumstances in the many Christian communities to which he writes.

A Man for All People

Paul was born a citizen of Tarsus in Cilicia, a region in the southeast part of Asia Minor—a part of modern-day Turkey. Here Jewish studies flourished in the midst of the Greek world. The circumstances of Paul's life provide him with a rich and diverse background. He is influenced by three different spheres: he is a Jew, a Greek, and a Roman—providing him the ideal position from which to bring the message of Jesus Christ to the great cities of his day.

First and foremost, Paul is a Jew. He proudly proclaims that he is "an Israelite, a descendant of Abraham, of the tribe of Benjamin" (Rom 11:1). His Hebrew name is Saul, named after Israel's first king. Living in Tarsus, Paul is a member of what is called "diaspora Judaism"; that is, those Jews living outside Israel, scattered throughout the world. Judaism was a noteworthy religion within the empire, and synagogues could be found in most of the major cities throughout the Mediterranean world. Paul follows the Judaism associated with the Pharisees, which was centered on the synagogues and relied on the teachings of the rabbis. In the diaspora such things as circumcision, Sabbath laws, and food laws help to maintain Jewish identity and pass it on to the next generation.

Paul loves the Torah, and like most Jews he considers following its teachings a joy and privilege rather than a burden. As Acts tells us, he studied for a time in Jerusalem with the great rabbi Gamaliel (Acts 22:3). This gives him an excellent knowledge of the Hebrew Scriptures and the Jewish oral tradition, filling him with zeal for his ancestral religion. But Paul comes to realize that the Torah cannot overcome sin. While the Torah is God's gift, it cannot bring people to salvation.

Paul understands Christianity not as a new religion, but as the fulfillment of Judaism, as a new and complete way of understanding the religion of his ancestors. The Messiah has come, and so he knows that the end of the age is here. Yet, he is very clear about the fact that God's covenant with Israel has not been rejected. In his longest letter, Paul states the matter most certainly: "I ask, then, has God rejected his people? Of course not! . . . For the gifts and the call of God are irrevocable" (Rom 11:1, 29). Paul always remained a proud member of his ancient faith and understood his mission within the context of its inspired Scriptures.

Second, Paul is also a Greek, and his world is that of Hellenistic culture. Since the days of Alexander the Great, Greek has been the second language and the framework of thought for everyone reached by his conquests. Because Paul is a native of Tarsus, a great center of Greek learning, he not only speaks Greek, in addition to Hebrew and Aramaic, but Greek culture, philosophy, and rhetoric enrich his mind and his viewpoint. When he quotes from the ancient Scriptures in his writings, he uses the Greek translation, the version known as the Septuagint. With this translation of the Old Testament, Paul takes the word of God not only to the diaspora Jews but also to the Gentiles throughout the world.

The Greek world is characterized by a great variety of religious thought. The old religions of the national and city gods are losing their appeal, and there's a great thirst for a personally satisfying religion, a faith that could give meaning to life. In the Greek world, people of many different origins and traditions come into contact with one another creating both diversity and tension. The message that Paul preaches is a faith that gives life meaning and that brings unity to people. As he writes, "Here there is not Greek and Jew, circumcision and uncircumcision, barbarian, Scythian, slave, free; but Christ is all and in all" (Col 3:11).

And third, Paul lives as a citizen of Rome, a privilege he gains through his family and often uses to his advantage throughout his missionary work. Because Rome rules the world from east to west, a period of relative peace has been established in which commerce and culture may flourish. Roads crisscross the empire and the seas are made safe for passage, making it possible for Paul to travel throughout the Mediterranean world, preaching the gospel and establishing churches.

Paul, however, is not an uncritical inhabitant of the empire of Caesar. The cult of emperor worship and the massive power of the empire to crush those who try to interfere with its absolute authority are strong contrasts to the way of Christ. In the face of the imperial propaganda proclaiming Caesar as savior and lord of the world, Paul's gospel message is defiantly subversive. Yet, Paul sees no intrinsic conflict between being a Christian and a citizen, and he urges Christians to be good citizens of the Roman government. Ironically, at the end of his journeys, Paul will be killed in the Roman persecutions.

Paul describes himself as a man who has become "all things to all" (1 Cor 9:22). He uses his global, multicultural setting and mindset for the sake of the universal gospel he proclaims. Paul is a man who can talk with rabbis on the streets of Jerusalem and with philosophers on the streets of Athens. He understands the ancient wisdom of the Hebrew Scriptures, and he appreciates the wisdom of Greek literature, such as that found in the works of Homer, Sophocles, and Plato. But Paul also knows that the whole world—Jewish, Greek, and Roman—has been transformed and renewed in light of the death and resurrection of Jesus Christ. And he recognizes that his whole life pales in comparison to the highest good—that of knowing Christ.

> Circumcised on the eighth day, of the race of Israel, of the tribe of Benjamin, a Hebrew of Hebrew parentage, in observance of the law a Pharisee, in zeal I persecuted the church, in righteousness based on the law I was blameless.
>
> [But] whatever gains I had, these I have come to consider a loss because of Christ. More than that, I even consider everything as a loss because of the supreme good of knowing Christ Jesus my Lord. (Phil 3:5-8)

Paul proclaims a gospel expressed through the Scriptures and symbols of Israel (the Torah and the temple), through the language and worldwide thought patterns of Greece (philosophy and rhetoric), using the communication and transportation systems of Rome to his advantage. He travels up to the temple in Jerusalem for the feasts of Israel, and he journeys along the Roman roads to all parts of the known world. He proclaims that the God of Israel is the Creator and Sustainer of the whole world, and therefore he becomes a man for all people in order to bring the very Jewish message of the gospel to all the nations of the world.

Proclaiming Salvation to All the Nations

In his experience on the road to Damascus, Paul comes to know the risen Lord in a personal way that transforms his heart in a radical way. But it takes many years for Paul to learn how to express his new faith in the kind of pastoral language that we read in his letters. So, after his experience on the road, Paul does not immediately begin his evangelizing ministry. He tells us that he spent three years in Arabia and then went back to Damascus before he ever went to Jerusalem to confer with the apostles of Jesus.

> But when [God], who from my mother's womb had set me apart and called me through his grace, was pleased to reveal his Son to me, so that I might proclaim him to the Gentiles, I did not immediately consult flesh and blood, nor did I go up to Jerusalem to those who were apostles before me; rather, I went into Arabia and then returned to Damascus.
>
> Then after three years I went up to Jerusalem to confer with Cephas and remained with him for fifteen days. (Gal 1:15-18)

Many have assumed that Paul went eastward into Arabia to preach the gospel there. I believe it is more likely that he spent a period of prayerful reading of Scripture in that barren land. Although Paul knows the ancient texts of the Torah and prophets well, he must study them again because they have been fulfilled in

Israel's Messiah. In the light of the risen Lord, Paul finds fuller meaning in the Scriptures of Israel.

God has revealed to Abraham that he will "become the father of a multitude of nations" (Gen 17:4) and that in his descendants "all the nations of the earth will find blessing" (Gen 22:18). The prophets and sages of Israel have taught that, while God sustains a special relationship with Israel, his rule extends to the entire universe. God's Servant will play a decisive role in bringing God's salvation to all people. God has said to his Servant, "I will make you a light to the nations, / that my salvation may reach to the ends of the earth" (Isa 49:6).

In the light of Paul's listening again to God's word to Israel, he becomes convinced that Jesus dies on the cross so that in him "the blessing of Abraham might be extended to the Gentiles" (Gal 3:14). He sees that God's ancient desire to bring salvation to the nations is being fulfilled in Jesus, God's Servant and Messiah.

Although Paul always remains a Jew, he spearheads the church's outreach to the peoples of the world, breaking down barriers between Jews and Gentiles. The transformation of a messianic movement within Judaism into the global church is in no small measure due to the mission, teachings, and letters of Paul.

United Together in Christ

We live in Christ; Christ lives in us. We are united with Christ through faith in his saving cross and resurrection. This union with Christ is the heart of Paul's teachings. Crucified with Christ, the old self dies, and in his resurrection, we live a new life.

> So whoever is in Christ is a new creation: the old things have passed away; behold, new things have come. (2 Cor 5:17)

This new life involves a new way of seeing, a new way of being, a new way of living—in reality, a new identity. To be "in Christ" means to live as a "new creation." As a new creation "in Christ," we are incorporated into the saving community, the body of Christ. This is a community in which boundaries that divide people are broken down, in which distinctions among people no longer matter.

In Paul's day, the world was divided between Jews and Gentiles, slaves and free people, women and men. But Paul envisions a Christian community that not only includes all of these but also brings them together into interdependent relationships. Part of the dramatic witness of the church of the first century is this attractive, alternative community of dissimilar people called into a higher unity in Christ.

Paul's first hint to us that he is addressing a transnational church comes in the greeting he offers at the beginning of all thirteen of his letters. "Grace and peace to you" is a remarkable combination of a Greek salutation *charis* (grace) and the ancient Hebrew blessing *shalom* (peace). Grace expresses the joyful fullness of the gospel and peace expresses the fullness of well-being that God desires for us. In this unique greeting, Paul addresses Gentile and Jewish believers together, as members of one church.

Notice that Paul does not write, "*Charis* to you Greeks and *shalom* to you Hebrews." Grace is not just for Gentiles and peace is not just for Jews. God desires the whole body of Christ to receive his grace and to experience his peace. Paul writes with respect for his readers' own ethnic and cultural backgrounds, yet he points to a new countercultural reality—a community in which the barriers between Jews and Gentiles is broken down and eliminated.

Writing to congregations that were often divided and torn by factional strife, Paul's greeting is a concrete reminder to believers that they are called to be a "new creation." While affirming the diversity of every part of the church, Paul transcends their differences to forge a new identity. The church is not a congregation created by simply linking Jews and Gentiles together but a united body of Christ, a transformed people made new in the risen Lord.

Because Paul is a boundary breaker, always seeking to remove the barriers that divide people from one another and from God, he teaches us that the church must be a boundary breaker too. When we listen to Paul, we discover possibilities that can transcend our differences of ethnicity, race, class, and gender and join us into a common unity.

As Paul speaks to us, he speaks a message of "grace and peace." When we extend grace to others and make peace with one another, we become boundary breakers, and, in so doing, we offer a powerful witness of Christ to our world.

 Paul frequently asked his congregations to **"imitate" him** (see 1 Cor 4:16; Phil 3:17). Paul viewed himself as a model for faith. Just as he attempted to emulate Jesus in every way, such as in embracing suffering and preaching good news, so Paul exhorted his communities to do likewise. Sometimes he commended their effectiveness in becoming models themselves (see 1 Thess 1:6-7).

The Letters of Paul

When Paul wrote he followed the normal style for letters written in his day. First comes the identification of the author followed by the name of the recipient of the letter. Next is the salutation or greeting. This is usually followed by a prayer or thanksgiving. Then comes the body or principal content of the letter, followed by the final greeting and farewell.

The content of his letters is derived from several different sources. Paul's insights come first of all from his years of reflection on the Scriptures of Israel. Second, his insights result from contemplating his experience of Christ on the road. Also, Paul knows the tradition about Jesus that has been handed down to him from others, especially from the original apostles. And finally, his letters are filled with insights gained from his missionary and pastoral experience.

These letters reveal many of Paul's personal characteristics and a fair amount about his life. In them we find a man of passionate zeal and deep love for Christ and the people of his churches. Chronologically speaking, his letters are penned closer to the historical events of Christ's earthly life than the gospels. Because of them, Paul is rightfully called the church's first theologian.

Providentially, after Paul's martyrdom, his followers collected his letters, edited them, and published at least some of them. By the end of the first century, his letters were being read in churches throughout the empire, and they made an enormous impact on Christian thought.

Nowhere does Paul write a methodical exposition of his teaching. His letters are forged in the midst of travel, change, and controversy. Usually we are reading only one side of an ongoing conversation between Paul and the people in whichever church he addresses. Our challenge is always to consider the circumstances that gave rise to his teaching and to discerningly separate his contingent advice from his permanent doctrine.

Paul's letters do not appear in the New Testament in the order in which they were written. Rather they are arranged generally according to length, from the longest, Romans, to the shortest, Philemon—with the nine letters to the churches first and the four letters to individuals afterward.

The groupings we will use are a traditional way of clustering these thirteen letters. First we look at what are called the Great Letters: Galatians, Romans, First and Second Corinthians. We also find the Eschatological Letters: First and Second Thessalonians. The Captivity Letters include Philippians, Philemon, Colossians, and Ephesians. And, finally, the Pastoral Letters: First and Second Timothy and Titus.

Paul's Letter to the Galatians

The first of the Great Letters, Paul's letter to the Galatians, is filled with intense emotion, frustration, and anger. Paul writes against the backdrop of the most heated controversy of the early church. Some in the community are teaching that Christianity is a form of Judaism and that anyone who wishes to become a Christian must first be converted to Judaism and observe all the prescriptions of the Jewish law. Others are teaching that Judaism is irrelevant for the Christian life. As a Jew, Paul knows that belief in Jesus Christ is rooted in Judaism, but he passionately defends the belief that Gentiles become Christians through faith in Christ and not by following the works prescribed in Israel's Torah.

Paul writes his letter to several church communities that he founded throughout the region of Galatia in Asia Minor. Apparently after Paul had left these communities, other missionaries came to them preaching a different message. These so-called false teachers, or Judaizers, demand that Christian converts submit to circumcision and to the dietary prescriptions of the Jewish law. Paul denounces them as preaching a false gospel and accuses them of undermining the meaning of Christ's saving work.

In this letter Paul offers us a glimpse into his own emotional life and convictions. In the first two chapters, he defends his authority as an apostle and offers his account of a meeting with Peter, James, and John in Jerusalem. Here Paul received the mandate for his mission. He is entrusted with the gospel to the uncircumcised (that is, the Gentiles) just as Peter has been entrusted with the gospel to the circumcised (that is, the Jews).

In the central section, Paul develops the primary theme of his letter—Christian freedom. Before the coming of Christ, the Mosaic law had been like a guardian for God's people in their youth. But now it is clear that in Christ all are children of God with full rights of inheritance.

> Before faith came, we were held in custody under law, confined for the faith that was to be revealed. Consequently, the law was our disciplinarian for Christ, that we might be justified by faith. But now that faith has come,

we are no longer under a disciplinarian. For through faith you are all children of God in Christ Jesus. (Gal 3:23-26)

Paul says that a child does not have to earn what is already freely given. Our inheritance as God's children is the salvation given to us by God through Christ.

In the final chapters, Paul discusses the practical consequences of this new freedom for the Christian life. It is not a license to do as we please. True freedom, rather, consists in serving one another through love (Gal 5:13), being guided by the Spirit (Gal 5:18), and seeking the fruit of the Spirit (Gal 5:22).

Paul's Letter to the Romans

Paul's letter to the Romans is his longest and most developed writing. As Paul pens this monumental letter to "all the beloved of God in Rome," he is writing to a church that he neither founded nor visited. Unlike his other letters, in which he writes to communities who know him well and addresses pastoral concerns of those churches, he writes here to the Christians in a city he has never seen.

He writes to the church in Rome primarily to prepare them for his intended visit. Paul has carried out his task of preaching in the eastern Mediterranean world, and now he is ready to undertake the proclamation of the gospel in the western half of that world. He hopes to make Rome, the imperial capital of the Roman world, the base of his future mission. This letter is both his personal introduction to the church in Rome and an exposition of his understanding of the gospel and the theology he has developed to date.

This gospel for which Paul is sent has been "promised previously" by God "through his prophets in the holy scriptures" (Rom 1:2). Throughout history the constant energy of God's love has been lighting up the darkness, desiring to bring salvation to the lost. The good news of Jesus Christ is the goal of Israel's long history as described in the ancient Scriptures.

Apart from him, all that God has done is incomplete. The prophets have communicated God's promise of a final liberation, and now God has spoken his final word, the gospel of Jesus Christ.

Paul's foundational premise is that all people are under the domination of sin: "All have sinned and are deprived of the glory of God" (Rom 3:23). Throughout the letter Paul uses the singular "sin" rather than the plural "sins." Sins are actions and attitudes that arise out of us; sin is the root and cause of these within us. Sins are the symptoms; sin is the disease. Sin is separation, alienation, division—from God, from one another, and from ourselves. It dwells within us and prevents us from being who we are created to be.

What Paul says about sin is weighed against a power that he calls grace. Grace is a free gift from God. It is acceptance, reunion, reconciliation. Sin is not simply something we do; grace is not simply something we have. Both have to do with our relationship to God; they both describe our very being. Sin leads to death; grace to life. Paul proclaims the good news that "where sin increased, grace overflowed all the more, so that, as sin reigned in death, grace also might reign through justification for eternal life through Jesus Christ our Lord" (Rom 5:20-21).

God has reconciled people with himself through Christ's sacrifice. This reconciliation unites the world back to God, it recovers a lost wholeness and integrity, and it creates again a right relationship between the Creator and creatures. It is pure gift; not something that can be earned or merited through observing the law. And it is through this gift of God that salvation has become available for everyone.

Although humanity stands justly condemned, God's final verdict is not condemnation but acquittal. And we take possession of this reconciliation with God through a relationship of "faith in Jesus Christ." This faith implies an acceptance of what we have received and the acknowledgment of Christ's lordship in our lives. It leads to a dedication and a commitment to Christ that progressively intensify.

In this jubilant text, Paul summarizes the divine process that leads to our salvation.

> Therefore, since we have been justified by faith, we have peace with God through our Lord Jesus Christ, through whom we have gained access [by faith] to this grace in which we stand, and we boast in hope of the glory of God. Not only that, but we even boast of our afflictions, knowing that affliction produces endurance, and endurance, proven character, and proven character, hope, and hope does not disappoint, because the love of God has been poured out into our hearts through the holy Spirit that has been given to us. For Christ, while we were still helpless, yet died at the appointed time for the ungodly. Indeed, only with difficulty does one die for a just person, though perhaps for a good person one might even find courage to die. But God proves his love for us in that while we were still sinners Christ died for us. How much more then, since we are now justified by his blood, will we be saved through him from the wrath. Indeed, if, while we were enemies, we were reconciled to God through the death of his Son, how much more, once reconciled, will we be saved by his life. Not only that, but we also boast of God through our Lord Jesus Christ, through whom we have now received reconciliation. (Rom 5:1-11)

Faith, a term rooted in the Old Testament, is a firm and unshakable trust. In the Old Testament faith means trusting in God's promises of future deliverance; in the New Testament faith means trusting that God has already delivered us in Jesus Christ, that in his death and resurrection we have God's final and definitive act of salvation. This personal trust and acceptance of God's gift also implies obedience to the way of salvation, acceptance of the cross as the way to resurrection and life, and submission to the demands of this new life that Christ gives.

Paul knows from his own experience that God's grace within us is strong enough to give us peace and hope even in the midst of adversity. Of course, "affliction" does not necessarily produce "endurance," and endurance doesn't always result in "proven character." Adversity often produces resentment and bitterness. But endurance, proven character, and hope are qualities of grace, and they develop when the believer stands reconciled before God and responds to affliction in faith.

The whole process of God's action on our behalf is rooted in God's love for us. In a way unparalleled by human love, God has given himself to us without restraint: "the love of God has been poured out into our hearts." The image is that of life-giving water being poured on thirsty land, torrential rains in an arid desert. God's love gushes forth into our hearts with abandon by the Holy Spirit.

It is impossible for us to understand the dimensions of divine love, but we see the manifestation of God's love in the death of his Son for us: "God proves his love for us in that while we were still sinners Christ died for us." God's love is unconditional love, independent of any worthiness or merit on our part. God's act of love is humanly inconceivable and contrary to all expectations, demonstrating beyond doubt God's personal love for us.

Paul's encouraging text is oriented toward the future when we will be "saved" through Christ. The peace and hope we experience in the present is just a foretaste of the fullness of salvation yet to come. We know in our hearts that we will experience the salvation that has been promised to us. The process of salvation will be complete when we share "the glory of God," the full image and likeness of God as our Creator intends. In faith we trust God completely to finish the work of our salvation and bring us to the glory he has promised.

Women Who Worked with Paul

The last chapter of Romans lists many people whom Paul greets, among them women who participated in his ministry. Phoebe is mentioned explicitly as a "deacon" (masculine form) in the church at Cenchreae, one of the ports of Corinth. The title clearly implies a ministry but one that is nowhere explained in detail. Junia is listed as "prominent among the apostles," but again there is little specificity to her exact ministry. That Paul had many female coworkers is clear, some of whom were heads of local churches.

Paul's Letters to the Corinthians

Corinth was a thriving port city, busy with travelers and traders going back and forth from east to west with commerce and ideas, a melting pot of cultures and religions. As the founder of the Christian community at Corinth, Paul continues to look after it as a father. As he tells the Corinthians, "I became your father in Christ Jesus through the gospel" (1 Cor 4:15). His two letters are one way in which he demonstrates his loving concern for his spiritual family.

In Paul's first letter, he refers to factions that have developed within the community since his departure. Paul urges the believers to unity by focusing not on human accomplishments, but on the cross of Christ.

> The message of the cross is foolishness to those who are perishing, but to us who are being saved it is the power of God. (1 Cor 1:18)

In the logic of human wisdom, the cross seems embarrassing and tragic. It expresses the ultimate in human weakness, failure, humiliation, and defeat. The gospel of a crucified Savior seems to be utter madness. Yet, in the crucifixion of his Son, God surpasses human wisdom and acts powerfully to save us from sin and death. Now the cross expresses radical giving for others, hope in the midst of suffering, and ultimate victory over the evil powers of sin and death.

Paul calls this mind-boggling paradox of the crucified Savior "the power of God and the wisdom of God." Here is truth that cannot be argued with reason or imposed with power. It has to be revealed by God, which is the reason that Paul has received his call to proclaim the gospel of the cross to an incredulous world longing for salvation.

Most of Paul's letters to the Corinthians are his responses to the questions and controversies that have arisen. They give us a glimpse into the life of this mid-first-century community as they struggle to live out their faith and baptism. Paul discusses marriage and celibacy, food sacrificed to pagan idols, headcovering for women, abuses when celebrating Eucharist, the use of spiritual gifts, and the resurrection of the dead. Some of the challenges that face the church in Corinth are universal and can be directly applied to our challenges today; others are pastoral responses that apply only to the church of first-century Corinth. Our challenge is to learn how to discern the message of the Scripture and respond to God's word today.

In Paul's second letter, he reveals more of himself than in any of his other letters. We see him in pain, in joy, in frustration, in decision, in anger, and in confidence. He writes frankly, and he writes affectionately. He speaks about his weakness and the hardships he has endured for the gospel, and marvels at the way God uses fragile, human instruments to communicate the treasure of the gospel.

> But we hold this treasure in earthen vessels, that the surpassing power may be of God and not from us. We are afflicted in every way, but not constrained; perplexed, but not driven to despair; persecuted, but not abandoned; struck down, but not destroyed; always carrying about in the body the dying of Jesus, so that the life of Jesus may also be manifested in our body. (2 Cor 4:7-10)

When holding the gospel as our treasure, our afflictions attest to our union with Christ, whose suffering and death is replicated in our own lives. We carry with us the dying of Jesus so that his life may be manifested in our mortal flesh. We carry an indestructible power that is not our own. Christ's life within us suffuses our present existence with visible signs of the resurrection for which we wait in hope.

Throughout the Mediterranean world, each church that Paul founded has its own particular problems and concerns, which were continually reported to him. Like a loving parent, Paul feels responsible for each

one. But travel is slow and distances are great. So his letters reveal the zeal of an evangelizer, the mind of a theologian, and the heart of a pastor.

As in the suffering of his Son, God uses Paul's hardships to make him a more perfect vessel of the gospel. Paul states the lessons he learns as a revelation from God: "My grace is sufficient for you, for power is made perfect in weakness" (2 Cor 12:9). This promise to Paul is made increasingly evident throughout his ongoing travels and even his imprisonments, which we will examine next.

CAPTIVITY, ESCHATOLOGICAL, AND PASTORAL LETTERS

As the great "missionary to the Gentiles" Paul travels far and wide to bring the gospel of Jesus Christ to new territories. He becomes the founder and shepherd of churches throughout the Roman Empire, as we read in the second half of the Acts of the Apostles. He considers both his personal presence and his letters from afar to be essential elements in the work of building up and encouraging these new churches.

These Pauline writings are quite distinct from the narrative writings of the four gospels and Acts. In each of these letters, Paul reflects on the ways that Jesus Christ is the fulfillment of God's promises in redemptive history and on the significance of his saving cross and resurrection. Paul also spends time in these writings on the implications of the salvation brought by Christ for the new life of believers. He both admonishes and encourages his readers according to the unique needs of each community to which he writes.

Paul's Captivity Letters

Four letters are traditionally described as Paul's Captivity Letters: Philippians, Philemon, Colossians, and Ephesians. These letters are joined by the fact that they each mention imprisonment as the context for Paul's writing. We know from Acts and his letters that Paul was imprisoned many times during his ministry: in Corinth, in Ephesus, in Caesarea, and in Rome. These letters could have originated in any of these locations. In these letters, despite his imprisonment, Paul expresses most clearly the freedom he experiences in Christ.

Paul's letter to the Philippians, the earliest of these letters from prison, is written to the community that Paul visited on his second and third missionary journeys. Paul explains how his imprisonment has served "to advance the gospel." Even though he is held in chains, his situation has encouraged others to take up the task, and now they "dare more than ever to proclaim the word fearlessly" (Phil 1:12-14).

Paul explains how the spiritual fruit of his captivity is joy, peace, and confidence. Although he is in dangerous circumstances, he is ready to live or to die because he knows that Christ will be glorified by either living or dying: "Christ will be magnified in my body, whether by life or by death." His immortal words are written over his tomb in Rome: "For to me life is Christ, and death is gain" (Phil 1:20, 21). Paul is totally confident in the Lord's power to bring good from suffering.

He urges the Christians in Philippi to conduct their lives in a way that is worthy of the gospel of Christ. Paul and the Philippians share in the same struggle as they suffer for Christ. He exhorts them to live with "the same mind, with the same love, united in heart," and to have among themselves "the same attitude" as that of Christ Jesus. This oneness with him will lead them to avoid selfishness and to consider the interests of others over their own (Phil 2:2-5).

Paul integrates into his letter a hymn of the early church, chanting the pattern of Christ's life from humiliation to exaltation. It radically contrasts the values of the ancient world, in which honor and power are all important, with the values of Christ. Not grasping at equality with God, Jesus radically humbles himself to a state of slavery, the lowest of the lowly.

Who, though he was in the form of God,
  did not regard equality with God something
    to be grasped.
Rather, he emptied himself,
taking the form of a slave,
coming in human likeness;
and found human in appearance,
he humbled himself,
becoming obedient to death, even death on a
  cross. (Phil 2:6-8)

Yet, the powerless Jesus is not the end of the hymn. For its second half exalts the triumphal Christ. The one who empties himself receives from God more power and honor than even an emperor could ever hope.

Because of this, God greatly exalted him
  and bestowed on him the name
  that is above every name,
  that at the name of Jesus
  every knee should bend,
  of those in heaven and on earth and under
    the earth,
  and every tongue confess that
  Jesus Christ is Lord,
  to the glory of God the Father. (Phil 2:9-11)

Paul reverses the imagery of the creation accounts. Adam, who was formed in God's image, grasped at equality with God. He was filled with pride and was ultimately brought low by God. But Jesus, "though he was in the form of God, / did not regard equality with God something to be grasped." He emptied himself, humbled himself, and took the form of a slave, but ultimately he was exalted by God.

Paul also reverses the vocabulary of imperial literature in which the emperor is proclaimed as Lord and honored with bended knees. The one who was crucified by the empire is now exalted with the divine title of Lord. He is worshiped not only by those in the Roman Empire, but the whole cosmos gives him glory and honor.

The most descriptive word for this letter is "joy." Although he writes from a prison cell, Paul rejoices at the continuing progress of the gospel and expresses his deep gratitude for the church in Philippi. He encourages the community to the highest standards in their life together:

> Rejoice in the Lord always. I say it again: rejoice! Your kindness should be known to all. The Lord is near. Have no anxiety at all, but in everything, by prayer and petition, with thanksgiving, make your requests known to God. Then the peace of God that surpasses all understanding will guard your hearts and minds in Christ Jesus. (Phil 4:4-7)

Paul's second Captivity Letter is his memo to Philemon. It is the shortest of Paul's letters, but we can be grateful that this small postcard was not lost. From prison Paul writes on behalf of Onesimus, a slave who has run away from his master but whom Paul has converted to Christ and baptized. Paul will send this letter with Onesimus back to his master.

Paul writes to the slave's owner, Philemon, and urges him to welcome Onesimus back—not as a slave but as a brother in Christ. Paul tactfully tries to balance his concern for the runaway slave with his regard for his master's legal rights and feelings. He writes: "Perhaps this is why he was away from you for a while, that you might have him back forever, no longer as a slave but more than a slave, a brother, beloved especially to me, but even more so to you, as a man and in the Lord" (Phlm 15-16).

Paul's appeal for the slave is filled with strong arguments and personal appeals, yet Paul never tells Philemon what to do. Although Paul could certainly order him "to do what is proper," he prefers to appeal to Philemon, urging him "out of love" (Phlm 8-9). Paul wants him to do the good in a way that is not forced but voluntary.

Paul is advocating for Onesimus because this slave is now a member of Christ's church. Paul refers to Onesimus as his "child" and himself as the slave's "father" (Phlm 10). He even offers to make good on the slave's debt: "If he has done you any injustice or owes you anything, charge it to me." And in a not-so-subtle appeal, Paul says, "May I not tell you that you owe me your very self" (Phlm 18-19). Although Paul offers to pay Philemon for the debt of the slave, Paul slyly reminds Philemon that he already owes him his eternal life. Paul had brought salvation to Philemon by introducing him to the Christian faith. Such debts can never be repaid.

Paul helps Philemon to acknowledge the profound difference between the Roman world of masters and slaves in which he lives and the community that followers of Jesus Christ are called to create. While Paul does not directly challenge the social institution of slavery, he convincingly shows that baptism into Christ creates a whole new way of looking at relationships between people. In Christ all distinctions of religion, race, gender, class, and nationality are insignificant. Unlike the patriarchal household, in the church all are one in Christ.

Philemon must realize for himself that he has joined a community called to make the standards of God's kingdom a reality already in this world. He must turn from the injustices prevalent in the sinful world to enter the new creation that Jesus Christ has established in his church.

Letters to the Colossians and Ephesians

The third Captivity Letter is addressed to the Colossians. Paul addresses a church besieged with the crosscurrents of many religious and philosophical ideas: mystery religions, eastern philosophies, gnosticism, astrology, and others. False teachers were leading the community astray by speaking about Christ as just one of a whole host of heavenly beings who were thought to rule the world.

Rather than confronting these problems directly, Paul urges the community to hold fast to the faith they were taught, not to be led astray and enslaved again. He articulates a true understanding of Christ that ought to permeate the minds and hearts of those who follow him. Through a beautiful hymn, he teaches them the orthodox belief that Christ is the fullness of God and Lord of the universe.

He is the image of the invisible God,
the firstborn of all creation.
For in him were created all things in heaven
and on earth,
the visible and the invisible,
whether thrones or dominions or
principalities or powers;
all things were created through him and for
him.
He is before all things,
and in him all things hold together.
He is the head of the body, the church.
He is the beginning, the firstborn from the dead,
that in all things he himself might be
preeminent.
For in him all the fullness was pleased to dwell,
and through him to reconcile all things for
him,
making peace by the blood of his cross
[through him] whether those on earth or
those in heaven.
(Col 1:15-20)

The hymn exalts the cosmic reality of Christ, praising him as superior to all other beings and asserting that all invisible powers are created through him and for him. As the "image of the invisible God," he is the one in whom all people encounter God. But not only is Christ exalted over all creation, he is also the risen One, the firstborn of the dead, the beginning and source of the final fullness that God desires. Through his sacrifice on the cross, he has reconciled heaven and earth and established the new creation. He now reigns as head of the cosmic body that is the church.

Paul continues to elaborate his teaching on the primacy of Christ. Against the deceptive arguments of false teachers, he encourages his readers to "walk in him, rooted in him and built upon him and established in the faith as you were taught, abounding in thanksgiving" (Col 2:6-7). He further admonishes the community to adhere to the gospel and to seek only Christ.

See to it that no one captivate you with an empty, seductive philosophy according to human tradition, according to the elemental powers of the world and not according to Christ.

For in him dwells the whole fullness of the deity bodily, and you share in this fullness in him, who is the head of every principality and power. (Col 2:8-10)

Then, as in most Pauline letters, Paul offers some practical advice and ethical implications for living concretely the Christian teaching he has proclaimed. If, indeed, Christ is the Lord of the universe and of our lives, then we must live fully in him. Paul offers lists of vices that believers must avoid followed by characteristics of "the new self," which must distinguish their lives being remade in God's image. The reality of Christ must define the lives of believers.

Let the word of Christ dwell in you richly, as in all wisdom you teach and admonish one another, singing psalms, hymns, and spiritual songs with gratitude in your hearts to God. And whatever you do, in word or in deed, do everything in the name of the Lord Jesus, giving thanks to God the Father through him. (Col 3:16-17)

The letter to the Ephesians, the fourth Captivity Letter, has a far more general and universal scope than the others. In the opening greeting, the destination "in Ephesus" is missing in most of the earliest manuscripts, leading some scholars to speculate that the letter was written as an encyclical, or circular letter, meant to be distributed to many churches in Asia Minor.

The opening prayer of praise succinctly sets forth the theme of the entire letter. The author gives praise to the God of Israel, whom he identifies as the "Father of our Lord Jesus Christ." God's grand plan of universal salvation, called here the "mystery" of God's will, has now been revealed.

In all wisdom and insight, he has made known to us the mystery of his will in accord with his favor that he set forth in him as a plan for the fullness of times, to sum up all things in Christ, in heaven and on earth. (Eph 1:8-10)

The revelation of this "mystery," God's master plan, which was hidden from past ages, is the unfolding of salvation history. Paul goes on to explain that this mystery is today being revealed by God through the Holy Spirit. The first critical step in God's cosmic goal is unity between Jews and Gentiles, which expresses the oneness of all humanity in Christ. This unity will be followed by the renewal of all created reality, eventually bringing all things to their perfection in Christ.

The church, as Paul describes it in Ephesians, is the universal church. It is the fullness of Christ: "[God] put all things beneath [Christ's] feet and gave him as head over all things to the church, which is his body, the fullness of the one who fills all things in every way" (Eph 1:22-23). Paul is saying that without the church, Christ would not be complete. To be sure, the church is Christ's very substance in the world. As the church grows and flourishes, the fullness of Christ is manifested.

This universal church is the divine instrument for making known God's plan for the salvation of the world. It is both the sign of God's saving will and the means for accomplishing it. In describing the church the letter uses several images that speak of its essential oneness with Christ. The church is called Christ's body, his bride, a holy temple, a city, a family household, and the people of God. It is one, holy, catholic, and apostolic. In this beautiful description of the church, we see our high calling as members of the church, as part of God's plan, chosen in Christ before the foundation of the world. As the Spirit works in the church, this mystery of God's unifying plan will continue to unfold to all generations.

After Paul describes the mystery of God's saving plan and its unfolding through Christ and his church, the second half of his letter urges Christians to live a life that is worthy of the mystery of God's plan. Namely, members of Christ's body must practice the virtues that make possible the church's harmony: humility, gentleness, patience, love, and peace. The church is able to be a witness and instrument of God's saving plan for the world when its members strive for unity.

I, then, a prisoner for the Lord, urge you to live in a manner worthy of the call you have received, with all humility and gentleness, with patience, bearing with one another through love, striving to preserve the unity of the spirit through the bond of peace: one body and one Spirit, as you were also called to the one hope of your call; one Lord, one faith, one baptism; one God and Father of all, who is over all and through all and in all. (Eph 4:1-6)

The unity of the church is rooted in the oneness of God, the ultimate source of unity. Paul describes the church as "one body" which is animated by "one spirit." This unified church strives toward its "one hope," the inheritance promised by the church's "one Lord." The church is united in the "one faith," the gospel it professes, and "one baptism," through which each member is initiated into the life of Christ. This series of seven facets of the church's unity culminates in the origin of its unity, the "one God and Father of all."

 Paul's image of the **"body of Christ"** for the church is one of the most important in the New Testament (cf. 1 Cor 12:12-27; Eph 1:22-23; Col 1:18). In the Greco-Roman world the "body" was identified both with the human body and a political reality, such as a city. When one part of the body suffers, all suffer. When another part rejoices, so do all. Vatican II featured this image prominently in calling the church to recognize the diversity within it while working for the deeper unity desired by Christ (*Dogmatic Constitution on the Church* 7, 17).

The Eschatological Letters

The two brief letters addressed to the Thessalonians may be called the Eschatological Letters. Eschatology is a technical term referring to the end-times and the glorious return of Christ. Paul writes these letters to correct misconceptions within the church in Thessalonica, which seems preoccupied with the end of the world.

The audience of the first letter is concerned that those who have already died will miss out on the blessings of the Lord's coming. Paul sets their minds to rest so they "may not grieve like the rest, who have no hope" (1 Thess 4:13). He assures them that, whether dead or alive at Christ's return, no believer will be at a disadvantage. Those who have died in Christ will rise from death and participate in his final triumph. Paul uses the imagery of trumpet blasts, the call of angels, and Christ's descent on the clouds, which are common ways of expressing the end-time in the religious literature of the times.

Many of the early Christians have a vivid expectation that the coming of Jesus will be soon, probably within the lifetime of many. Paul instills within the church a sense of waiting with anticipation, yet he also warns that we cannot name the day or control the circumstances. While Christ's coming can be trusted, it cannot be predicted. Paul uses the gospel images of the thief who breaks in at night and labor pains of pregnancy to describe the unexpected suddenness and inevitability of "the day of the Lord" (1 Thess 5:1-3).

The audience of the second letter is also preoccupied with the end-times. Many among them are alarmed and frightened about the coming of Christ, and some have even quit working because they are convinced that the day is imminent. Paul admonishes them not to be shaken by deceptive teachings, but he assures them that God has chosen them "as the firstfruits for salvation" (2 Thess 2:13). Paul's metaphor indicates that the Thessalonians are only the beginning of the full harvest of evangelization that God intends to gather.

The term "salvation" embraces the whole work of God in Christ on our behalf. Its implications are past, present, and future. God has called us through the gospel "to possess the glory of our Lord Jesus Christ" (2 Thess 2:14). That glory, which was manifested at Christ's coming into the world, is now experienced by believers through the Christian life. Then the complete manifestation of Christ's glory will be made at his return. Our full sharing in that glory will make our salvation complete.

In these Eschatological Letters, Paul instructs his readers to keep watchful, with one eye on the future and the other on the here and now. He urges them to be prepared always for the Lord, but he gives them lots of practical advice about keeping their lives in focus. The best preparation for the coming of the Lord is to be faithful and loving in daily responsibilities: "abound in love for one another" (1 Thess 3:12); "be blameless in holiness" (1 Thess 3:13); "refrain from immorality" (1 Thess 4:3); "console one another" (1 Thess 4:18); "stay alert and sober" (1 Thess 5:6); "encourage one another" (1 Thess 5:11); "admonish the idle, cheer the fainthearted, support the weak" (1 Thess 5:14); "pray without ceasing" (1 Thess 5:17); "test everything; retain what is good" (1 Thess 5:21); "let no one deceive you in any way" (2 Thess 2:3); "and hold fast to the traditions that you were taught" (2 Thess 2:15).

The Pastoral Letters

The three Pastoral Letters to Timothy and Titus form a distinct group within the Pauline writings. They are addressed not to churches in particular locations, but to two individuals—two of Paul's most faithful disciples—as they shepherd congregations. The letters are concerned with the organization and direction of the churches that Paul has entrusted to their care. These three letters help us understand the problems faced by the church as leadership passed from the apostles to the second generation of Christians.

The form and content of these letters suggest that they were written later than the other Pauline letters. If they were written by Paul before his martyrdom, they may have been written by a secretary or coauthor, a common practice at the time. Paul would have given them a fair amount of freedom in writing out his thought. Undoubtedly, too, Paul's own understanding of Christ and the church underwent change and maturing through the years, so that his vocabulary and ideas surely expanded in his later writings.

It is also possible that they were written in Paul's name by a disciple who interpreted Paul's teaching for a new time and context. Yet, even in this scenario, some parts of these letters may very well be Paul's composition, used by the writer as reminders of the unchangeable teaching and foundational ministry of Paul himself. But whether Paul wrote these letters himself, or whether he is simply the authority behind them, the important reality is that they are canonical Scripture written under the inspiration of God's Spirit in the tradition of the great apostle Paul.

These letters are "pastoral" for several reasons. First, they express concern for sound doctrine, and they warn against false teaching within the community of faith. Second, they express concern for community leadership and the orderly succession of those holding office within the church. Third, they express concern for apostolic tradition, for the faithful handing on of what the community has received from the apostles. These are the concerns of a church in transition. The older leaders of the church were dying and the church was spreading into new cultures. Clarifying teachings, confirming new leaders, staying firmly rooted in the tradition—these are the necessary means of strengthening the internal character of the church.

In the First Letter to Timothy, Paul first urges Timothy to restrain false teachers and be faithful to his appointed task.

> I entrust this charge to you, Timothy, my child, in accordance with the prophetic words once spoken about you. Through them may you fight a good fight by having faith and a good conscience. Some, by rejecting conscience, have made a shipwreck of their faith. (1 Tim 1:18-19)

Next, he gives regulations for correct conduct in the liturgical assembly and lists qualifications for leadership within the community. He describes the church as the "household of God" and "the pillar and foundation of truth" (1 Tim 3:15). Then Paul gives advice to Timothy for his teaching and his conduct.

> Do not neglect the gift you have, which was conferred on you through the prophetic word with the imposition of hands of the presbyterate. Be diligent in these matters, be absorbed in them, so that your progress may be evident to everyone. (1 Tim 4:14-15)

Finally, Paul gives practical advice concerning members of the community, especially for widows, presbyters, slaves, and masters. In his final exhortation, Paul counsels, "O Timothy, guard what has been entrusted to you" (1 Tim 6:20).

The Second Letter to Timothy is deeply personal and moving. It has the character of a final testament from Paul to his younger, beloved disciple. In a series of exhortations, he urges Timothy to remain faithful to what he has learned and believed, reminding him of the seriousness of his task. In his final exhortation, Paul presses his disciple to be constant, patient, and courageous, urging him to bear his share of the hardship that the gospel entails.

> I charge you in the presence of God and of Christ Jesus . . . proclaim the word; be persistent whether it is convenient or inconvenient; convince, reprimand, encourage through all patience and teaching. For the time will come when people will not tolerate sound doctrine but, following their own desires and insatiable curiosity, will accumulate teachers and will stop listening to the truth and will be diverted to myths. But you, be self-possessed in all circumstances; put up with hardship; perform the work of an evangelist; fulfill your ministry. (2 Tim 4:1-5)

The short Letter to Titus begins with the qualifications of a Christian leader, with special attention given again to the necessity to refute false teachings. Next, guidelines for Christian behavior are given, highlighting the responsibilities of various classes of people placed under the pastoral guidance of Titus.

All are urged to live peacefully with one another in response to the generous love of Christ.

> For the grace of God has appeared, saving all and training us to reject godless ways and worldly desires and to live temperately, justly, and devoutly in this age, as we await the blessed hope, the appearance of the glory of the great God and of our savior Jesus Christ. (Tit 2:11-13)

When Paul wrote his letters, he certainly had no idea that he would also be writing to us, two thousand years later. He had no idea how his words would direct the history of Christianity, much less that his writings would soon become the sacred Scriptures of the church. It is because the Holy Spirit, who guided the early church, also guides the church today that Paul's writings are as important today as they were for the first century.

Just because a work was written to meet the needs of an immediate situation does not mean, however, that it is temporary. All the great love songs of the world were written for one person, but they live on for all people. It is because Paul's letters were written with the passionate intensity of the immediate situation that they still speak powerfully to us today. It is because they were written to people seeking understanding of the good news they had just received that they still bring understanding and truth.

Because these writing are both time-bound and timeless, they present a continual challenge of interpretation for us. It would surely be a mistake for us to expect the church to speak and act today the same as the church in first-century Corinth or Thessalonica and to slavishly follow all the recommendations of Paul. Yet, we are the same church. And because the challenge to understand and proclaim the gospel is ceaseless, we can look to the inspired Pauline writings as a constant source of truth in a changing world.

EXPLORING LESSON THREE

1. Paul's conversion (or call) was the single most significant event in his adult life (see Acts 9:1-22; Gal 1:11-24), setting him on a new path of ministry and relationship with Christ. What event in your life has set you in a new direction or brought you closer to Christ?

_____

_____

_____

_____

2. How did being Jewish, Greek, and Roman help Paul in his missionary work?

_____

_____

_____

_____

3. In his letter to the Galatians, Paul responds to the most heated controversy of the early church. How would you summarize this controversy and Paul's response (Gal 2:15-16; 3:23-26; 5:6)?

_____

_____

_____

_____

4. What is the relationship between "sin" and "grace" as explained by Paul in his letter to the Romans (Rom 5:20-21; 6:12-14)?

_____

_____

_____

_____

5. The church in Corinth experienced many divisions and a sense of competition among its own members. Read 1 Cor 1:10-31. How does Paul use the cross of Jesus as a model of how the Corinthians should be and act?

_____

_____

_____

_____

6. In his letter to the Ephesians, Paul describes the church using a variety of images. Read Eph 2:19-22, a description of the church as "the household of God." In what ways does this description resonate with your own experience of church? Where might we, the church, grow in this identity as "household" or family?

_____

_____

_____

_____

_____

7. In his letters to the Thessalonians, what attitude(s) does Paul encourage as Christians wait for the return of Jesus (1 Thess 3:12-13; 5:6; 5:23; 2 Thess 2:15)?

_____

_____

_____

_____

_____

8. Read Paul's very personal advice to Timothy in 2 Timothy 4:1-5 as if it is addressed directly to you. Do you find it challenging or encouraging or both? How or in what circumstances are you being called to be an "evangelist" or a sharer of the good news of salvation in Christ?

_____

_____

_____

_____

_____

9. What new thing did you learn about this extraordinary missionary, theologian, and man of faith, the apostle Paul? Which of his letters would you be interested in reading and studying in more detail?

_____

_____

_____

_____

_____

CLOSING PRAYER

Prayer

If there is any encouragement in Christ, any solace in love, any participation in the Spirit, any compassion and mercy, complete my joy by being of the same mind, with the same love, united in heart, thinking one thing. Do nothing out of selfishness or out of vainglory; rather, humbly regard others as more important than yourselves, each looking out not for his own interests, but [also] everyone for those of others. (Phil 2:1-4)

Lord Jesus, your tireless apostle Paul traveled thousands of miles to share the good news of salvation with all who would listen, and to encourage all who believe in you to embrace your way of humility and love. Give us a share in your Spirit and unify us as your church so we too may tirelessly proclaim the wisdom and power of your cross with our lives. We pray for those who bear their own crosses this day, that they may do so with the mind and strength of Christ, especially . . .

LESSON FOUR

Other New Testament Writings

Begin your personal study and group discussion with a simple and sincere prayer such as:

Prayer

Jesus Christ, you are the Word that reveals the Father. As we study the good news of your life, death, and resurrection, may what you reveal to us take root in our hearts and give life to our church and to our world.

Read pages 78–91, Lesson Four.

Respond to the questions on pages 92–94, Exploring Lesson Four.

The Closing Prayer on page 94 is for your personal use and may be used at the end of group discussion.

HEBREWS AND THE CATHOLIC LETTERS

The letter to the Hebrews and the Catholic Letters represent an expression of early Christianity distinct from what we read in the Pauline letters. These writings, the monumental letter to the Hebrews and the other non-Pauline letters of the New Testament, are written by a variety of different authors in the early church. Although most of these writings were accepted only gradually by the early church into the New Testament, they are a treasure of material produced in the age of apostolic Christianity.

The seven Catholic Letters have very little in common with one another except that they are all known to us by the name of their author, rather than the person or community to whom they are addressed. They are called "catholic," which means universal, because the ancient interpreters considered them addressed to the whole church rather than to specific communities, as with the Pauline letters. The Catholic Letters are James, First and Second Peter, First, Second, and Third John, and Jude. We will look at four of them, since the letters of John are more appropriately grouped, as we saw earlier, with the Gospel of John.

The Letter to the Hebrews

Hebrews is written to a community of Christians who have become weary and discouraged and have begun to lose heart. They have been suffering under the weight of persecution, trials, and imprisonment. The refreshing springs that have watered their faith are drying up, and it becomes necessary to dig deeper to find springs of living water once again. The teachings in Hebrews are the result of digging deeper, to greater theological depths, in order to capture a renewed sense of who Jesus Christ is and what he means for our lives. Nowhere in Scripture do we find a more wondrous statement of what Christ has accomplished for us.

The author writes anonymously and ends the work by calling it a "message of encourage-

ment" (Heb 13:22). The form is more like a written homily, teaching and exhorting those who listen, to believe more vigorously and to carry on with renewed vitality in the challenges ahead. The homily, however, is often called a letter because the author gives it an epistolary ending (a closing like those typically found in letters) before sending it out to be read in the church's liturgy.

Hebrews is filled with characters, symbols, themes, images, and quotations from the Scriptures of Israel. The original audience would not have been able to understand its teachings or recognize its rich vocabulary without being deeply conversant with the ancient texts. For us, reading Hebrews is a powerful reminder that our Christian roots are in the Scriptures of Israel. The more we know the Old Testament—its heroes, its stories, and its institutions—the more we will understand this work.

Yet, the extensive use of the ancient texts serves only to focus our attention more intently on the person of Jesus Christ. As the opening verse says, "In times past, God spoke in partial and various ways to our ancestors through the prophets; in these last days, he spoke to us through a son, whom he made heir of all things" (Heb 1:1-2). The book continually teaches how the old gives way to the new. The people, experiences, and institutions of Israel are the essential foundation for what is final and definitive in Jesus Christ. The titles of Jesus given throughout the letter are all prefigured in the ancient Scriptures. Jesus is called Son, heir of all things, the firstborn, the high priest, apostle, forerunner, mediator of a new covenant, minister of the sanctuary, the leader and perfecter of faith, the great shepherd of the sheep, and Jesus our Lord.

Jesus is first compared with Moses. Moses is the mediator of the old covenant; Christ mediates the new covenant. Both are noted for their faithfulness in the house of God, which is God's people, but Christ is shown to be greater than Moses: "Moses was 'faithful in all his house' as a 'servant' to testify to what would be spoken, but Christ was faithful as a son placed over his house" (Heb 3:5-6).

Jesus is then compared to the priests in the line of Levi and to Melchizedek. The Levitical priesthood was a temporary office received through hereditary succession. The priesthood of Melchizedek, however, is a unique priesthood, not distinguished by ancestry and inheritance. Jesus is a priest like the ancient Melchizedek—an eternal, unchanging priest. The many priests of the old covenant give way to the everlasting priesthood of Christ.

> Those priests were many because they were prevented by death from remaining in office, but he, because he remains forever, has a priesthood that does not pass away. Therefore, he is always able to save those who approach God through him, since he lives forever to make intercession for them. (Heb 7:23-25)

The sacrifice of Christ is then compared with the Day of Atonement, the annual day of reconciliation offered at the temple of Jerusalem. After the animal sacrifices are offered for the sins of the people, the high priest of Israel enters into the Holy of Holies and sprinkles the animal blood to accomplish the atonement for the sins of the previous year. But the sacrifice of Christ, the eternal high priest, is not limited to the earthly world. Rather, he entered the sanctuary of heaven and accomplished the redemption of all.

> But when Christ came as high priest of the good things that have come to be, passing through the greater and more perfect tabernacle not made by hands, that is, not belonging to this creation, he entered once for all into the sanctuary, not with the blood of goats and calves but with his own blood, thus obtaining eternal redemption. (Heb 9:11-12)

The high priest of Israel exercises his ministry in the earthly temple; Christ makes atonement for sin in the perfect sanctuary of heaven. Offering the perfect sacrifice of his own body and blood, he removes the barrier of sin that has separated humanity from God. No further sacrifice ever need be offered because Jesus Christ is that eternal offering: "We have been consecrated through the offering of the body of Jesus Christ once for all" (Heb 10:10).

Solidarity with the Cloud of Witnesses

Hebrews discusses the nature of faith by presenting a long line of striking examples of faith and perseverance from the Old Testament (Hebrews 11–12) . The writer calls them a "cloud of witnesses"—heroes of faith that surround us and give us courage and inspiration. In offering these witnesses from of old, Hebrews offers a stirring summary of Israel's whole salvation history. Some of these heroes of faith are familiar to us—like Abraham, Sarah, Moses, and David. Others might not be so familiar—like Rahab, Gideon, Barak, and Jephthah. The writer's use of the Old Testament encourages us to turn to the ancient Scriptures, to learn the stories of our ancestors. Like the Christian communion of saints, they inspire us and support us on our journey.

Lest we think that the patriarchs, matriarchs, priests, and prophets of old are excluded from the assembly of heaven because of the failures of the first covenant, Hebrews assures us that these ancestors receive what has been promised them. Because of their faith, they share in the presence of God enabled by Israel's fulfillment in Jesus Christ. Together with them we are on a great pilgrimage to the heavenly

Jerusalem, "for here we have no lasting city, but we seek the one that is to come" (Heb 13:14).

The author continually alternates between instruction and exhortation. The central teaching of Hebrews is that Christ is our great high priest, offering his perfect sacrifice for sin, becoming mediator of the new and eternal covenant. But these doctrinal teachings give us incentive to live out their implications. The more we know God's word, the more we will be moved to live God's word. "The word of God," the author proclaims, "is living and effective, sharper than any two-edged sword" (Heb 4:12). God's word calls us, invites us, challenges us, and penetrates into our innermost being.

Hebrews presents Jesus not just as someone to inspire us from the past but as the high priest who continues to act in the present. Jesus is living and active now, interceding for us. "Today" is the time to focus on. As the author proclaims: "Jesus Christ is the same yesterday, today, and forever" (Heb 13:8). In him we share in a new way of existing. We have nothing to fear, not even death. So we are free to live fully, free to serve, free to experience all that God wants to share with us.

In so many ways we are like the original audience of Hebrews. So often we experience obstacles to faith. We get discouraged; we feel like we've lost the fire. This homily calls us to a deeper reflection on what Christ has done for us so that we will be given renewed faith and encouragement for the pilgrimage ahead.

The Letter of James

The letter of James begins with the salutation, "James, a slave of God and of the Lord Jesus Christ, to the twelve tribes in the dispersion, greetings" (Jas 1:1). We do not know with certainty the identity of James or of the twelve tribes in the dispersion. In the New Testament there are at least three important disciples named James. Two of them are members of the Twelve, and another is a relative of Jesus, usu-

ally called in the gospels "brother of the Lord." It is this third James who is traditionally associated with this letter. He is the leader of the church in Jerusalem after the departure of Peter, and he represents the Jewish Christian position in dialogue with Paul. This letter then is written either directly by this James or by his disciples in his name. The "twelve tribes" is a traditional title for the people of Israel. Since the church understands itself to be the new Israel, the "twelve tribes in the dispersion" probably refers to the Christian church scattered throughout the Roman Empire.

The writing is distinctively Jewish in character. It is filled with common sense advice about living our faith in the real world. It is primarily exhortation, and is written within the tradition of Israel's wisdom literature. Consisting of loosely connected moral advice, it is remarkably similar to the books of Proverbs and Sirach.

James offers guidance on many different ethical issues. He urges the community to persevere in times of trial and temptation because these are a testing ground for faith. He warns them against class distinctions that favor the rich and slight the poor. This kind of partiality, he says, is particularly detestable in the liturgical assemblies. He cautions his readers about the power of speech and how the tongue can be used for great good or great evil. Though the tongue is small, it has great power, like the rudder of a ship. He then challenges his readers to examine their motivations: to root out greed, jealousy, and worldliness from their hearts, and implant humility, patience, and mercy.

James continually urges Christians to realize that authentic faith is not just interior. He says, "Be doers of the word and not hearers only" (Jas 1:22). He urges them not only to talk the talk, but to walk the walk. James offers several examples from the Scriptures and from daily life to indicate the necessity of both faith and good works. Deeds done in love, he demonstrates, are not simply outward signs of faith; they are, rather, faith itself in action. These works reveal the depths of a faith that strives to imitate the faith of Jesus. He says, "See how a person is justified by works and not by faith alone. . . . For just as a body without a spirit is dead, so also faith without works is dead" (Jas 2:24, 26)

The teachings of James and the teachings of Paul seem to be contradictory. Paul says, "A person is justified by faith apart from works of the law" (Rom 3:28). James says, "A person is justified by works and not by faith alone" (Jas 2:24). But the understanding of the church has developed by listening to both voices. By placing both Paul and James in the canon of Scripture, the church refuses to adopt one to the exclusion of the other.

I suspect that James and Paul would have no problem with the teachings of one another. James was probably responding to those who misunderstood and distorted the teaching of Paul. Both Paul and James know that the foundation of a Christian life is faith. Faith for Paul means believing the truth of the gospel, trusting in God's power, and obeying God's will; or as he says in Galatians, "faith working through love" (Gal 5:6). Paul's point is that nothing we can do on our own can earn God's gift of salvation. But anyone who would say all you have to do is relax and believe, without manifesting that belief in loving actions, would earn the condemnation of both of these great writers. Faith is genuine only when it is expressed in loving deeds for others.

The teachings of James reflect the covenantal demands found in the Torah and the prophets. Sharing possessions with the poor, paying just wages to workers, and caring for orphans and widows, James exhorts his readers, are all actions that reflect a living faith. Anyone who acts in ways contrary to the injunctions of the Torah and prophets reveals an empty faith.

James presents Abraham as a "friend of God," as one whose orientation toward God leads him to see his own life through God's eyes and to obey. If Abraham had been oriented toward the world, he would have considered God's call to offer his son on the altar to be meaningless. In Abraham, "faith was ac-

tive along with his works, and faith was completed by the works" (Jas 2:21-23). Likewise, James tells us all that no one can be "of two minds," desiring friendship with God and friendship with the world at the same time. Our deeds will manifest the basic orientation of our lives.

The author of the letter of James challenges a believing community to **integrate faith and action**. This teaching presupposes the incarnation of Jesus and a sacramental worldview. Because God became human in Jesus and because material things like oil, water, bread, and wine bear the divine presence, human well-being is an integral dimension of Christian faith. The Second Vatican Council exhorted Christians "to perform their duties faithfully in the spirit of the Gospel. It is a mistake to think that, because we have here no lasting city, but seek the city which is to come, we are entitled to evade our earthly responsibilities according to each one's vocation. . . . One of the gravest errors of our time is the dichotomy between the faith which many profess and their day-to-day conduct" (*Pastoral Constitution on the Church in the Modern World*, 43).

The First Letter of Peter

The First Letter of Peter begins with the salutation from Peter the apostle to Christian communities located in the five provinces of Asia Minor (today's Turkey). If the letter is from Peter himself, then Peter writes it from Rome shortly before his martyrdom there (AD 64–68), although he authors it with the help of his secretary who is mentioned at the end of the letter: "I write you this briefly through Silvanus, whom I consider a faithful brother" (1 Pet 5:12). Silvanus gives written expression to Peter's thought in his own cultivated Greek style. If the letter was written after Peter's death, it serves as a short compendium of Peter's teachings, written in his name by one of his disciples. Possibly Silvanus himself composed the letter using Peter's earlier letters and sermons as sources. In either case, the letter represents a magnificent statement of Peter's apostolic zeal for the believers in distant lands.

Peter's letter demonstrates the strong bonds that united the early Christian communities stretched out across the world. From the church in Rome, Peter reaches out to the small towns in the remote provinces of Asia Minor through this letter designed to be circulated among them. As Christians, their values and goals placed them at odds with the predominant society around them. Peter writes to build up their faith and to help them face the challenges of living as believers surrounded by hostility. He reminds them that they are not alone but are part of a worldwide church united together in suffering and in hope.

Although this letter is written to communities composed primarily of Gentiles, Peter strives to keep Christianity within the framework of ancient Israel to make sure that its Jewish character is not lost. The letter is permeated with quotations, allusions, and images from the Scriptures of Israel. The letter shows how Peter integrates his Jewish faith with his reflection on the teachings, sufferings, death, and resurrection of Jesus. Now all believers are God's chosen people, Jews and Gentiles united in Christ, the fulfillment of God's purposes from the beginning.

According to God's grand design for the church, we are like "living stones" being built upon the foundation stone of Jesus into a spiritual temple offering spiritual sacrifices: "Like living stones, let yourselves be built into a spiritual house to be a holy priesthood to offer spiritual sacrifices acceptable to God through Jesus Christ" (1 Pet 2:5). As individual believers are built up in faith, each one becomes an integral part of God's house, according to the divine architectural plan. This holy temple exists for the singular purpose of worshiping God. In contrast to the temple of ancient Israel, made

of lifeless stones, this spiritual house is made of living stones. Rather than an inherited priesthood made up only of Levites, all Christians form a holy priesthood. Instead of material sacrifices, Christians offer spiritual sacrifices of prayer and praise, of self-consecration and self-giving. Such sacrifices are acceptable to God not on account of the one offering them, but because they are made "through Jesus Christ," that is, joined with his perfect sacrifice and united with his Spirit.

The writer emphasizes the new birth and new hope given in Christian baptism. He has incorporated fragments of hymns, creeds, and elements of the church's baptismal liturgy into this letter. Through baptism, believers come to share in the paschal mystery—the suffering, death, and resurrection of Christ. Like their ancestors who were freed from slavery through the waters of the sea, they are now God's people.

> You are "a chosen race, a royal priesthood, a holy nation, a people of his own, so that you may announce the praises" of him who called you out of darkness into his wonderful light.
>
> Once you were "no people"
>   but now you are God's people;
> you "had not received mercy"
>   but now you have received mercy.
>   (1 Pet 2:9-10)

Christians live their baptismal call in the midst of the world. While separate in spirit from the world, they are nevertheless instructed to participate in the world and the structures of human society. In this way, the Christian is able to participate in God's work of moving the world toward its final destiny. The secular world, in the eyes of the Christian, is a sacred world—a world that needs a message of hope, a world destined for transformation and glory.

> The end of all things is at hand. Therefore, be serious and sober for prayers. Above all, let your love for one another be intense, because love covers a multitude of sins. Be hospitable to one another without complaining. As each

one has received a gift, use it to serve one another as good stewards of God's varied grace. (1 Pet 4:7-10)

The final section of the letter consists of a series of imperatives: humble yourselves, cast all your worries on God, keep sober and alert, and resist your opponent, the devil (1 Pet 5:6-9). Despite the suffering of the present age, God still remains in control of events. Because the devil is constantly prowling like a ferocious lion, we must oppose him, but not with our own power. We must stand firm in our faith, because our adversary is conquered only with the power of Christ. God is using every experience, especially that of suffering, to further his loving purposes in our lives and to enable us to grow in grace. Because we know that God cares personally about all his people, we can rely on God's power to deliver his own when the time is right.

The Second Letter of Peter and the Letter of Jude

The Second Letter of Peter is significantly different in tone and content from the first letter. Most scholars assert that it was written in the name of Peter, probably well after Peter's death. By identifying himself with Peter, the author witnesses to the reverence for Peter held in the early church and indicates his intention to transmit and defend apostolic teaching.

The letter reflects the fact that the early church understood its mission to preserve the teachings received from the apostles and to refute false teachings. The writer struggles to persuade his readers to turn away from "false prophets" and "false teachers" who introduce "destructive heresies" (2 Pet 2:1).

The fundamental error condemned in this letter is the belief that there will be no second coming of Christ—no Parousia—and thus no final judgment. Since Christ has not returned in glory during the first generation of Christians, some are teaching that the world will remain the same rather than moving toward any final destiny. The writer, backed by sound tradition coming from the apostles, affirms the Lord's promise that he will come again, but not on their timetable.

> But do not ignore this one fact, beloved, that with the Lord one day is like a thousand years and a thousand years like one day. The Lord does not delay his promise, as some regard "delay," but he is patient with you, not wishing that any should perish but that all should come to repentance. But the day of the Lord will come like a thief, and then the heavens will pass away with a mighty roar and the elements will be dissolved by fire, and the earth and everything done on it will be found out. . . .
>
> But according to his promise we await new heavens and a new earth in which righteousness dwells. (2 Pet 3:8-10, 13)

The writer urges readers to be prepared for the Lord's coming and the new creation that God will establish. He calls upon the teachings of Peter, as well as the letter of Jude, and the authority of Paul's writings to rebut the false ideas recently introduced into the community.

The short letter of Jude begins with the salutation: "Jude, a slave of Jesus Christ and brother of James, to those who are called, beloved in God the Father and kept safe for Jesus Christ" (Jude 1). This Jude is most probably the brother of James of Jerusalem, the source of the letter of James. Nothing else is known about this Jude, thus the need to identify him by reference to his better-known brother. Those addressed by the letter are described in general terms, perhaps because the letter is addressed to all Christians.

The letter is an urgent note written to warn the churches against false teachers. Though we don't know the exact nature of the errors, we do know that the author vehemently condemns the falsehood and urges the churches to remain faithful to what was handed down by the apostles. Much of the letter is very similar to the Second Letter of Peter, and it is generally agreed that the letter of Jude is earlier.

The letter concludes with a majestic prayer of praise, probably taken from the liturgy of the early church.

> To the one who is able to keep you from stumbling and to present you unblemished and exultant, in the presence of his glory, to the only God, our savior, through Jesus Christ our Lord be glory, majesty, power, and authority from ages past, now, and for ages to come. Amen. (Jude 24-25)

Reading the many letters of the New Testament is like pulling out old yellowed family letters from the back of a desk drawer. On reading them we are reminded of people and times long since past. But we are also amazed at how much some things never change—the same struggles, the same hopes, in every generation. We see in them some fresh wisdom that gives insights for our challenges today. We realize again that these are family letters. And when we read them in a spirit of prayer and reflection, we share in the faith and the hope of our ancestors in the apostolic age. The inspired wisdom of their age becomes the wisdom of God for us.

 A passage from Second Peter is the earliest evidence that **Paul's letters could cause misunderstanding** because of their complexity: "In them [the letters of Paul] there are some things hard to understand that the ignorant and unstable distort to their own destruction, just as they do the other scriptures" (3:16). The author warns against personal interpretation of Paul's writings (see 1:19-21) by those less qualified than himself. The passage hints that Paul's letters already may have circulated widely among Christians as important documents to preserve, thus providing the impetus for the formation of the New Testament itself.

THE BOOK OF REVELATION

It is most appropriate that the book of Revelation has been chosen by the church to be the last book of the Bible. As the Bible begins with God's creation in the book of Genesis, it ends with God's new creation in Revelation. The work demonstrates that Jesus Christ is the summit of salvation history. As the book proclaims, he is "the Alpha and the Omega, the first and the last, the beginning and the end" (Rev 22:13). Christ is the originator of the universe—through him all things were made; and he is the goal of the universe—through him all things are fulfilled.

More than in any other book of the New Testament, the author incorporates a wide range of Old Testament texts and themes: the Genesis story of the temptation and fall, the Exodus account of the plagues and rescue, the historical books describing Israel's temple and worship, the Wisdom writings, and the words of the prophets. The author communicates the reality that the whole of Scripture—the Torah, the Prophets, and the Writings—is illuminated with new and fuller meaning in the light of Christ. What God has been doing throughout the history of salvation is fulfilled and coming to its climactic completion.

Apocalyptic Writing for a Church in Crisis

Revelation is written in a literary form called "apocalyptic," a type of religious writing common among Jews and Christians of the first century. The apocalyptic form includes many of the elements that make Revelation seem so bewildering—mysterious visions, strange combinations of symbols, and cryptic numbers. The early Christians were familiar with apocalyptic writing and its symbols, so they knew how to read the book. But these elements combine to make the book of Revelation seem obscure and unapproachable for us.

People in our day are intrigued when told by literalists that the inspired Bible contains predictions about what is going to happen in the future, about coming wars, and about the nations and politics of the world. In fact, throughout history people have attempted to use this book to forecast what would happen in their own century, and there are countless people today who want to use Revelation to promote sensationalism.

But when Revelation is interpreted as a book only about the future, it is open to endless misinterpretation and distortion. We must realize that the work does not give predictions about future events; much less does it give a timetable for the end of the world. Rather, it is introduced as a "prophetic message" (Rev 1:3) that its readers must heed. Like the prophetic writing of Israel, it proclaims the word of God in the midst of the challenges of the present situation.

The apocalyptic form is crisis literature. It is designed to bring a message of hope and consolation to those who are in the midst of a desperate condition. Whether or not the author imagined the book speaking to people in the future, he directs his writing to the people of his own day. The Christian communities of the late first century are experiencing great suffering from persecution. Revelation, like the gospels, is a book of good news—the glad tidings of Jesus Christ, of him who suffered and died yet has risen in victory. The good news assures Christ's followers that if they hold fast to him in their suffering, they will share in his victory.

Because Revelation is a Christian apocalyptic book, it proclaims to God's people that all they have been hoping for has already been achieved. The triumph over evil, sin, and death has been accomplished in the cross and resurrection of Jesus. The victory has been won, yet the world awaits its complete realization. The paschal mystery of Christ continues to unfold in the life of individual Christians as they follow in the way of the cross. Though we will have tribulation in the world, we know that in Christ we can have confident assurance.

Reading Revelation as a Liturgical Text

As the book begins, John the author describes himself as exiled "on the island called Patmos," a small rocky island in the Aegean Sea. He is held there as a prisoner because of his witness to Jesus. From there he writes this text addressed to seven churches in Asia Minor.

Worship is a large part of the content and context of Revelation. The liturgical images and actions that pervade the book are derived from both the young tradition of Christian eucharistic worship in the first century and the ancient tradition of Israelite temple liturgy. John's visionary experiences occur on a Sunday, the Lord's day, probably in the midst of the eucharistic liturgy.

> I, John, your brother, who share with you the distress, the kingdom, and the endurance we have in Jesus, found myself on the island called Patmos because I proclaimed God's word and gave testimony to Jesus. I was caught up in spirit on the Lord's day and heard behind me a voice as loud as a trumpet, which said, "Write on a scroll what you see and send it to the seven churches: to Ephesus, Smyrna, Pergamum, Thyatira, Sardis, Philadelphia, and Laodicea." (Rev 1:9-11)

The content of many of John's visions are experiences of the heavenly liturgy: the slain and glorified Christ offering himself to the Father while all the hosts of heaven bow in worship. Whenever the church's liturgy is celebrated, earth and heaven are joined. The earthly liturgy is a reflection of the eternal liturgy of heaven.

In this central action of both heaven and earth, the past, present, and future merge. The eucharistic assembly is, at the same time, a present experience of Christian worship, a re-enactment of Jesus' death and resurrection, and an anticipation of the messianic banquet at the end of time. As John enters the church's liturgy on Patmos, he is united with the crucified and risen Christ, with the angels and the saints as they offer praise in heaven, and with the seven churches to whom he writes.

The churches to which Revelation is sent are all found in Asia Minor, in the western part of modern-day Turkey. They are separated from one another by about a day's journey. Seven

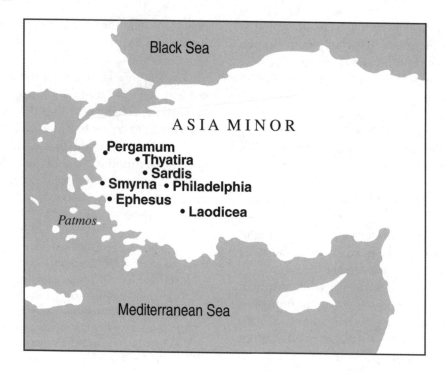

messages are given to the seven churches. These seven are historical communities, but since they are seven in number (a symbol for wholeness), they also represent the whole church. In the tradition of the prophets of Israel, the words to each community are harsh and critical, as well as encouraging and comforting.

Each of the seven churches reads this text of Revelation in their Sunday assembly. In the lamp-lit darkness as the Christians gather to worship, they listen to the words of John and engage in his visionary experiences. As the word is proclaimed, they meet the risen Christ, participate in the heavenly liturgy before God's throne, witness the attack of the ancient dragon, and experience the deepest meaning of Christ's conquest through his saving death.

As the worshipers engage as participants in the battle of Christ against the beast, they are transformed from victims of oppressive circumstances to victors with Christ over the ultimate forces of evil. The reading of Revelation in the context of worship enables the listener to experience the one "who is and who was and who is to come" (Rev 1:8). Christ's timeless and universal offering of himself for the salvation of the world becomes present at every time and in every place the Eucharist is celebrated. This present offering to the Father, joining earth and heaven, is a foretaste and preparation for the complete manifestation of Christ's reign and the completion of his saving work in the new creation.

The liturgical acclamation of the Christian assembly, "Come, Lord Jesus," is a prayer for the present moment as well as for the ultimate future. Gathered around the Lord's table, the assembly hears the response of Jesus, "I am coming soon" (Rev 22:20), a coming already made known in the past, a coming anticipated in the future "day of the Lord," and a coming that is experienced now in the present—forming the communities of the seven churches into faithful witnesses of Christ and victors in union with him.

Reading the Symbolic Language

One of the keys to interpreting Revelation is unlocking the symbols. In human communication, symbols allow us to express what cannot be completely expressed in straightforward speech. Our most cherished convictions find their expression in symbolic images and actions. Think of the cross, the flag, your ring. Symbols affect us at a level deeper than intellectual understanding. They do not simply communicate information; they take hold of us and elicit powerful emotions and convictions.

Revelation is not a codebook; it is a symphony of images. It is important that we read it with our imaginations engaged. Attempts to express images and symbols in logical, factual language rob them of their rich meaning and power of persuasion. Revelation should be approached more like a work of art than a mathematical problem. Interpreting symbolic language is less a rational act than an act of the imagination.

We can gain hints at the meaning of the book's many symbolic numbers, colors, places, and creatures by understanding the meaning of similar symbolism in other parts of the Bible and other first-century Jewish and Christian literature. For example: the color white represents Christ's resurrection; red represents evil; gold, divinity. The secret of the numbers can begin to be unlocked when we realize that seven represents totality; four signifies the whole world; 1000 signifies immensity; twelve refers to Israel and the church founded on the twelve tribes and the twelve apostles.

In the opening vision, Jesus appears in majesty. He wears the robe of a priest, and the golden sash of a king. His hair is white, his face shines like the sun, his eyes are flaming, and a two-edged sword comes forth from his mouth. The description connects Jesus with the messianic writings of the Hebrew prophets. The author combines prophetic references in new ways, and demonstrates that Jesus is the perfection of all that has been done by the priests and kings of Israel. He has the characteristics of the eternal God from the prophetic writings, and he is shown to be the universal judge of the earth. He holds seven stars in his right hand and stands in the midst of seven golden lampstands, representing the seven churches addressed in the book.

When I caught sight of him, I fell down at his feet as though dead. He touched me with his right hand and said, "Do not be afraid. I am the first and the last, the one who lives. Once I was dead, but now I am alive forever and ever. I hold the keys to death and the nether world. Write down, therefore, what you have seen, and what is happening, and what will happen afterwards. This is the secret meaning of the seven stars you saw in my right hand, and of the seven gold lampstands: the seven stars are the angels of the seven churches, and the seven lampstands are the seven churches." (Rev 1:17-20)

The author combines these symbolic elements to create powerful literary images. These symbolic descriptions are not to be taken literally or to be pictured realistically. In a later image of Christ, the author further elaborates his symbolic system.

Then I saw standing in the midst of the throne and the four living creatures and the elders, a Lamb that seemed to have been slain. He had seven horns and seven eyes; these are the seven spirits of God sent out into the whole world. He came and received the scroll from the right hand of the one who sat on the throne. When he took it, the four living creatures and the twenty-four elders fell down before the Lamb. (Rev 5:6-8)

The lamb, of course, represents Christ throughout the book. He is "the Lamb of God," as designated in John's gospel. He appears to have been slain, though he is standing—a symbolic proclamation of his sacrificial death and resurrection to life. The horn is a traditional symbol for power; thus the seven horns show that the power of Christ is total and complete. The eyes represent knowledge, so the seven eyes signify Christ's universal understanding.

There follows in the book a series of sevens: seven seals, seven trumpets, and seven bowls poured out. Each of them reveals apocalyptic signs and terrors, showing a spiraling progress leading up to the revelation of the new creation, the kingdom of God, in the final chapters. Here Christ is imagined as a divine warrior coming on his white horse. He is called "Faithful and True," "Word of God," and "King of kings and Lord of lords." Having conquered all obstacles, he comes to claim his bride and to celebrate the royal wedding, which will secure his kingdom forever. The bride, clothed in fine linen and adorned in royal splendor, is the church. She comes to meet her royal bridegroom, and the great wedding feast of the Lamb begins.

Revelation gives us the imagination to see the whole world with sacramental vision, to know that Christ truly reigns over the world and its future. Revelation does not literally predict future events. The warnings given by biblical writings are always offered for the purpose of conversion; they are offered in order to change God's people. For example, when Jonah went through the city proclaiming God's prophetic word, "Forty days more and Nineveh will be overthrown" (Jonah 3:4), God's threatening word was designed to bring the people to repentance. And when the city turned from its evil ways, God did not inflict the calamity his prophet had proclaimed to them (Jonah 3:10).

God cannot be imprisoned in a predetermined script. Jesus has told us that figuring out the world's future in detail is not God's will for us. He has told us that only the Father knows about the day or the hour (Mark 13:32) and that he will come like a thief (Rev 16:15), without warning or expectation. Revelation is not about *what* the future holds, but about *who* holds the future. Once we have glimpsed the world in this way, then the hope that we are given inspires us to commit ourselves to the values of Christ, to work for a more peaceful world, to labor for the healing and reconciliation of people, and to see everyone around us as sacred and beloved of God.

The **four living creatures** of Revelation 4 who worship God day and night are said to resemble a lion, a calf, a human being, and an eagle (a clear reference to Ezek 10:14). Although these creatures originally symbolized what is noblest, strongest, wisest and swiftest in creation, very early in the Christian tradition, they came to be associated with the four canonical gospels. The human being is Matthew, the lion is Mark, the calf (traditionally translated "ox") is Luke, and the eagle is John.

The Choice between the Lamb and the Beasts

"The Lamb" appears twenty-eight times in the book of Revelation, always as a rich verbal icon of Jesus Christ. The author draws upon the rich heritage of Israelite and Christian imagery in depicting Christ as God's Lamb. Already in the first book of the Bible, Abraham assures his son Isaac that God will provide the lamb for the sacrifice. All of salvation history is really a waiting for the Lamb that God would give to his people. In the story of Exodus, the Israelites sacrifice the Passover lamb on the night of their liberation. The blood of the lamb on their doorposts frees them from destruction so they can journey to the land promised to them.

In explaining the meaning of Christ's sacrifice, the early Christians looked to the Scriptures of Israel. Isaiah describes the Suffering Servant, a figure who suffered vicariously for God's people, as afflicted and wounded, "like a lamb led to slaughter" (Isa 53:7). John's gospel sums up the ancient sacrificial images of the Old Testament when he calls Jesus "the Lamb of God, who takes away the sin of the world" (John 1:29, 36); and Paul uses the same imagery when he calls Jesus "our paschal lamb" who has been sacrificed (1 Cor 5:7).

In Revelation, the Lamb is triumphant, but bearing the marks of his sacrifice, "a Lamb that seemed to have been slain" (Rev 5:6). He is given honor and glory by the angels and saints of heaven, and he is followed by the one hundred and forty-four thousand, who have "washed their robes and made them white in the blood of the Lamb" (Rev 7:14; 14:4). He conquers the beasts that make war on him

(Rev 17:14) and his victory is celebrated on "the wedding day of the Lamb" (Rev 19:7-9).

In opposition to the richly developed image of the Lamb, biblical literature borrows from the mythological literature of the ancient Near East to express the reality of chaos and evil in the symbolic form of beasts. In the Old Testament these primordial beasts represent the powers that threaten God's people. In the book of Job, Leviathan is the repulsive serpent in the sea and Behemoth is an ox-like beast on the earth (Job 40:15–41:34). Throughout the Scriptures of Israel, beasts represent the powers of Israel's enemies, especially the might of Egypt and Babylon. In the visions of Daniel, the great empires of the world and their rulers are depicted as grotesque and ferocious beasts that make war on the people of the earth (Dan 7).

In Revelation, "beast" is used thirty-nine times to refer to the enemies of God's people. The ultimate figure of evil is the fiery red dragon, with seven heads, ten horns, and a destructive tail. The beast that arises from the sea combines all the characteristics of the four beasts in Daniel's vision, thus representing all the political powers that oppress and dehumanize. It receives its authority from the dragon and the whole world worships it. The beast that arises from the land is deceptive, possessing horns like the lamb and speaking like the dragon. It is called the "false prophet" and causes the earth's inhabitants to worship the beast from the sea. The mark of this beast, the number 666, is a distorted imitation of the protective seal placed on the foreheads of God's people.

The dragon and its two allied beasts form what some authors have called "a counterfeit trinity." The dragon, the source of all evil, is an anti-God. The first beast, which receives its authority from the dragon, is an anti-Christ. The second beast, which promotes the worship of the anti-Christ beast through trickery, is an anti-Spirit.

Like the Israelites renewing the covenant in the promised land were commanded, "Choose today whom you will serve" (Josh 24:15), the people of the earth must choose between the Lamb and the beasts. There can be no peaceful coexistence between the worshipers of the satanic dragon and his beastly allies on the one hand and those worshiping God and the Lamb on the other. "Choose today whom you will serve" is the imperative of the book of Revelation. Counterfeit trinities continue to draw people in every age to offer their allegiance to movements and ideologies that distort God's will for individuals and for the world. The reign of darkness continues to oppose the kingdom of God.

Most importantly for this last book of the Bible, however, we must know that the Lamb has conquered the beasts. Not only does Revelation proclaim that Christ conquers the empires and global powers that tyrannize and oppress people, the book announces that Christ conquers evil itself and casts it forever into the fiery pit of destruction. The consequence of our choice for the Lamb is nothing less than a share in God's newly created and perfected world.

Recapping the History of Salvation

Revelation reiterates the Bible's drama of salvation through the richly symbolic form of apocalyptic literature. The two focal events of Scripture, the exodus of the Old Testament and the paschal mystery of the New Testament, are expressed anew and linked to the lives of the Christians of the seven churches. Through vivid imagery drawn from both testaments, the author expresses the full results of God's liberation of the Israelites from Egypt and the saving death and resurrection of Jesus Christ.

Imagery from the story of the exodus fills the visions of Revelation. The seven seals, seven trumpets, and seven bowls echo and intensify the plagues brought against Pharaoh in the exodus. Hearing the cry of his suffering people, God threatened Egypt with a series of afflictions as part of his overall goal of liberating his people from injustice. The plagues serve for the conversion of the oppressor and the liberation of God's people.

This helps us understand that the threatened tribulations that fill Revelation are designed to bring about repentance, not to inflict cruelty. The dreadful series of plagues is not a coded script of what is to come in the future, but a frightening warning to bring God's people to repentance and to wake us up. They exhort us to choose God's vision of life rather than the terrible but inevitable consequences of violent oppression.

The people of God continue to experience a new exodus throughout history. In the first century the Christians addressed in John's visions are threatened by the agonies of the beasts, the violent oppression at the hands of the Roman Empire. Jesus is both the new Moses, leading his people to new life, and the Passover Lamb, the sacrificial victim whose blood was shed for their liberation.

The song of Moses, the victory hymn sung by the Israelites after they crossed the sea into freedom, has become in Revelation the song of the Lamb, sung in praise of God's deliverance after the conquest of the beasts (Rev 15:3).

Revelation is above all a retelling of the story of the death and resurrection of Jesus using new imagery. The heart of the gospel is told in a new way, through the daring form of apocalyptic literature. The book expresses the cosmic significance of the paschal mystery of Christ's sacrificial death and glorious resurrection, presenting it as a fundamental battle between the forces of good and evil. It is about the struggle of Jesus with the evil powers of this world, their unremitting destruction of him, and his ultimate vindication. The images of Christ throughout—the heavenly human being of chapter 1, the slain-yet-standing Lamb of chapter 5, the newborn son of the heavenly woman of chapter 12, and the triumphant rider on the white horse of chapter 19—all express different facets of the crucified and glorified Christ. They are multiple ways of expressing the meaning of Christ's saving victory in apocalyptic form.

The redemption achieved through the exodus of Israel from slavery and the death and resurrection of Christ are already experienced by people on earth, but the complete saving effects of God's victory are not yet fully manifest in the world. In the present time, we are living in the time between the glorification of Christ and his final coming to make all things new. Revelation lifts the veil that covers our eyes during this time of anticipation so that we can see the full significance of our salvation. It gives us glimpses, through highly symbolic language, of the full effects of liberation on God's people and the risen life that Christ has won for us.

The Matrimonial Union of Christ and His Church

Revelation increasingly draws us into the vision of the new creation. We are called back to the Genesis world of paradise where God, at the culmination of creation, made the woman. As God brought the woman to the man and presented her as his bride, their union in love is the crown of God's creation—the very image of God.

It is the goal of humanity to become the full image of God, to become a bright and shining manifestation of God's glory. This is the new creation, presented in Revelation in images of matrimonial union. Renewed humanity is united to Christ, and the bride is married to the King of kings—the perfect union for which all the earth has been longing.

> Then I saw a new heaven and a new earth. The former heaven and the former earth had passed away, and the sea was no more. I also saw the holy city, a new Jerusalem, coming down out of heaven from God, prepared as a bride adorned for her husband. I heard a voice from the throne saying, "Behold, God's dwelling is with the human race. He will dwell with them and they will be his people and God himself will always be with them as their God. He will wipe every tear from their eyes, and there shall be no more death or mourning, wailing or pain, [for] the old order has passed away." (Rev 21:1-4)

The book of Revelation, like each book of Scripture, speaks to us today as its truth endures from age to age. In our battles against evil, sin, death, and despair, we know that the victory has been won in the dying and rising of Christ. We are a people of hope because the one who died on the cross is the one whose power and riches, wisdom and strength, honor and glory and blessing last forever.

Like the early Christians, we experience the sharp conflicts between good and evil, the Lamb and the beasts. We live in the midst of a society in which superficial materialism, unbridled consumerism, and self-centered individualism stand opposed to the values of God's kingdom. Suffering and persecution is still frequent for those seeking to promote the gospel in our world.

Hope and confidence in the future, provided by all Scripture as it terminates in Revelation, gives us inner strength and the ability to go on. Through this inspired book we know that the link between the sometimes painful present and the glorious future is the resurrection of Jesus Christ. He is the basis for all our hope.

The book of Revelation is a good example to illustrate a truth that applies to the whole of the Scriptures. We will never have all the answers; we will never completely understand it all. Above all, don't get frustrated with what you don't comprehend, and don't think you can ever answer every question that arises from your prayerful reading and study. Learn to live with the mystery of God's word. Rejoice in the insights you gain; savor the people, stories, and events that fill your mind and heart from the Bible.

The Bible is like a bottomless well, from which we can always draw refreshing waters. In this panorama we've drawn up a couple of buckets-full, but there is so much more. The more of God's living water we drink, the more we will want. The wonderful thing about the Bible is that there will always be more to drink.

As we end this panorama of the Bible, let our prayer be that at the end of the book of Revelation: Maranatha—Come, Lord Jesus. Come to us, Lord, with your spirit of wisdom and understanding, so that we can know you more fully. Come to us with your spirit of encouragement and perseverance, so that we can follow in your way. Come to us with your spirit of love, so that our hearts may burn with love for you. Come to us in your holy Word. Come to us in the sacrament of Eucharist. Come to us as we exchange words with one another and as we break bread together. Come, Lord Jesus, come.

EXPLORING LESSON FOUR

1. Why are the New Testament books of James, First and Second Peter, Jude, and First, Second and Third John, and Jude called "catholic" letters?

_____

_____

_____

_____

_____

2. The author of the book of Hebrews provides a rich context for the life, death, and resurrection of Christ. Review a few of the references that illustrate how Christ fulfills the Scriptures of Israel (e.g., Heb 3:5-6; 7:23-25; 9:11-14; 10:11-12). How might the book of Hebrews help us as Christians be more aware of our Jewish roots?

_____

_____

_____

_____

_____

3. What is the benefit of reading about the "cloud of witnesses" (Heb 11:1–12:3) that have gone before us as examples of faith? Who would you include in your own personal "cloud of witnesses"—family members, friends, saints, others?

_____

_____

_____

_____

_____

4. The book of James insists that Christians must live out their faith in concrete ways: "Be doers of the word and not hearers only" (Jas 1:22). Evaluate how well you think we as a church are doing at following James' advice. How does your own parish or community live out this Christian maxim? What about you as an individual?

_____

_____

_____

_____

5. The author of Second Peter insists that Christ will indeed return in glory (2 Pet 3). Do we really live in expectation of Jesus' return? How can we maintain a lively sense of anticipation though so many years have passed since the first coming of Jesus?

_____

_____

_____

_____

6. a) What is the purpose of apocalyptic literature?

_____

_____

_____

b) In what sense is the book of Revelation a "prophetic message" (Rev 1:3)?

_____

_____

_____

7. What are some of the reasons that the author of Revelation uses "lamb" imagery to describe the crucified and risen Christ? (See Rev 5:6-14; 7:14; 13:8; 14:4; 17:14; 19:7-9 and Isa 53:7; John 1:29, 36; 1 Cor 5:7.)

_____

_____

_____

_____

8. Revelation, like all apocalyptic literature, offers hope to a weary people—hope in God's triumph, God's faithfulness, and God's steadfast love. Read and reflect on Rev 21:1-4.

a) Is this a description of an entirely future reality, or is it in some way already a present reality?

_____

_____

_____

b) How would you explain to others your belief in the nearness of God to human beings?

_____

_____

_____

9. As you reflect back on this panoramic study of the New Testament, what are some key thoughts or ideas that remain with you? What have you learned? What would you like to learn more about?

_____

_____

_____

_____

CLOSING PRAYER

Prayer

"*Worthy is the Lamb that was slain*
to receive power and riches, wisdom and
strength,
honor and glory and blessing."   (Rev 5:12)

Lamb of God, you are worthy of our praise. You are both slain and risen, wounded and victorious. As we await your return in glory, give us hearts like yours. Grant us some share in your wisdom and strength. And above all, make us fertile ground for the triumphant, faithful love you have offered your people yesterday, today and forever. We pray today for those who need to be strengthened in your triumphant love, especially . . .

PRAYING WITH YOUR GROUP

Because we know that the Bible allows us to hear God's voice, prayer provides the context for our study and sharing. By speaking and listening to God and each other, the discussion often grows to more deeply bond us to one another and to God.

At *the beginning and end of each lesson* simple prayers are provided for individual use, and also may be used within the group setting. Most of the closing prayers provided with each lesson relate directly to a theme from that lesson and encourage you to pray together for people and events in your local community.

Of course, there are many ways to center ourselves in God's presence as we gather together in groups around the word of God. We provide some additional suggestions here knowing you and your group will make prayer a priority as part of your gathering. These are simply alternative ways to pray if your group would like to try something different from those prayers provided in the previous pages.

Conversational Prayer

This form of prayer allows for the group members to pray in their own words in a way that is not intimidating. The group leader begins with Step One, inviting all to focus on the presence of Christ among them. After a few moments of quiet, the group leader invites anyone in the group to voice a prayer or two of thanksgiving; once that is complete, then anyone who has personal intentions may pray in their own words for their needs; finally, the group prays for the needs of others.

A suggested process:
In your own words, speak simple and short prayers to allow time for others to add their voices.

Focus on one "step" at a time, not worrying about praying for everything in your mental list at once.

Step One	Visualize Christ. Welcome him. Imagine him present with you in your group. Allow time for some silence.
Step Two	Gratitude opens our hearts. Use simple words such as, "Thank you, Lord, for . . ."
Step Three	Pray for your own needs knowing that others will pray with you. Be specific and honest. Use "I" and "me" language.

Step Four	Pray for others by name, with love.
	You may voice your agreement ("Yes, Lord").
	End with gratitude for sharing concerns.

Praying Like Ignatius

St. Ignatius Loyola, whose life and ministry are the foundation of the Jesuit community, invites us to enter into Scripture texts in order to experience the scenes, especially scenes of the gospels or other narrative parts of Scripture. Simply put, this is a method of creatively imagining the scene, viewing it from the inside, and asking God to meet you there. Most often, this is a personal form of prayer, but in a group setting, some of its elements can be helpful if you allow time for this process.

A suggested process:

- Select a scene from the chapters in the particular lesson.
- Read that scene out loud in the group, followed by some quiet time.
- Ask group members to place themselves in the scene (as a character, or as an onlooker) so that they can imagine the emotions, responses, and thinking that may have taken place. Notice the details and the tone, and imagine the interaction with the Lord that is taking place.
- Share with the group any insights that came to you in this quiet imagining.
- Allow each person in the group to thank God for some insight and to pray about some request that may have surfaced.

Sacred Reading (or Lectio Divina)

This method of prayer invites us to "listen with the ear of the heart" as St. Benedict's rule would say. We listen to the words and the phrasing, asking God to speak to our innermost being. Again, this method of prayer is most often used in an individual setting but may also be used in an adapted way within a group.

A suggested process:

- Select a scene from the chapters in the particular lesson.
- Read the scene out loud in the group, perhaps two times.
- Ask group members to ponder a word or phrase that stands out to them.
- The group members could then simply speak the word or phrase as a kind of litany of what was meaningful for your group.
- Allow time for more silence to ponder the words that were heard, asking God to reveal to you what message you are meant to hear, how God is speaking to you.
- Follow up with spoken intentions at the close of this group time.

REFLECTING ON SCRIPTURE

Reading Scripture is an opportunity not simply to learn new information but to listen to God who loves you. Pray that the same Holy Spirit who guided the formation of Scripture will inspire you to correctly understand what you read, and empower you to make what you read a part of your life.

The inspired word of God contains layers of meaning. As you make your way through passages of Scripture, whether studying a book of the Bible or focusing on a biblical theme, you may find it helpful to ask yourself these four questions:

What does the Scripture passage say?
Read the passage slowly and reflectively. Become familiar with it. If the passage you are reading is a narrative, carefully observe the characters and the plot. Use your imagination to picture the scene or enter into it.

What does the Scripture passage mean?
Read the footnotes in your Bible and the commentary provided to help you understand what the sacred writers intended and what God wants to communicate by means of their words.

What does the Scripture passage mean to me?
Meditate on the passage. God's word is living and powerful. What is God saying to you? How does the Scripture passage apply to your life today?

What am I going to do about it?
Try to discover how God may be challenging you in this passage. An encounter with God contains a challenge to know God's will and follow it more closely in daily life. Ask the Holy Spirit to inspire not only your mind but your life with this living word.